Dear Reader,

I must admit, I had a hard time leaving Silver Peak. This was my first time writing about Sadie and the rest of the folks in her community, and I wanted to just linger over coffee at Arbuckle's. But the mystery was solved, and it was time to move on. It's been a wonderful journey.

I typically write Christian historical romance set in the Regency era, so writing a contemporary mystery was a bit of a stretch for me. I don't do well with puns—the humor in Regency novels is usually quite arch—so I had to wing it with Sadie's love of jokes. On the other hand, it was great fun to incorporate all the elements of the historical mystery. I love the 1920s and 1930s, and I enjoyed having the chance to write about old movies, which are my favorites. I loved creating the character of Collin Malloy and giving him some of the elements of the old matinee idols that I watch all the time—men like Bing Crosby or Rudy Vallee.

I also enjoyed bringing Sadie and her grandchildren together on the scavenger hunt, and getting the whole town involved. Wouldn't it be lovely to live in a town just like Silver Peak?

I hope you enjoy *Time Will Tell* as much as I enjoyed writing it. Happy reading!

Blessings,
Lily George

Mysteries of Silver Peak

A Mountain of Mystery
Nobody's Safe
Silver Surprise
Wildfire
A Lode of Secrets
Time Will Tell

Time Will Tell

CAROLE JEFFERSON

Guideposts
New York

Mysteries of Silver Peak is a trademark of Guideposts.

Published by Guideposts Books & Inspirational Media
110 William Street
New York, New York 10038
Guideposts.org

Copyright © 2014 by Guideposts. All rights reserved.

This book, or parts thereof, may not be reproduced, stored in a retrieval system, or transmitted in any form or by any means, electronic, mechanical, photocopying, recording or otherwise, without the written permission of the publisher.

The characters and events in this book are fictional, and any resemblance to actual persons or events is coincidental.

Acknowledgments

Every attempt has been made to credit the sources of copyrighted material used in this book. If any such acknowledgment has been inadvertently omitted or miscredited, receipt of such information would be appreciated.

Scripture quotations are taken from *The Holy Bible, New International Version*. Copyright © 1973, 1978, 1984, 2011 by Biblica, Inc. Used by permission of Zondervan. All rights reserved worldwide. www.zondervan.com

"Discovering Silver Peak" by Jon Woodhams originally appeared in *Guideposts* magazine. Copyright © 2014 by Guideposts. All rights reserved.

Cover and interior design by Müllerhaus
Cover art by Greg Copeland represented by Deborah Wolfe, Ltd.
Typeset by Aptara, Inc.

Printed and bound in the United States of America
10 9 8 7 6 5 4 3 2 1

Time Will Tell

Prologue

Nathan Flats, the speediest delivery boy in Silver Peak—at least that was how he advertised himself to the growing number of folks who hired him—skidded to a halt a block from the opera house. His heart pounded against his rib cage as he tried to catch his breath. He'd just sneaked a peek at the pocket watch the folks at the jewelry store had trusted him to deliver. After all, a fellow didn't have the chance to see a real diamond-covered watch every day. Not in Silver Peak, anyway. And not in this ol' Depression. He'd just take a gander at it, and then he'd run it right over to where that big opera star, Collin Malloy, would be performing.

Gee, he might even have the chance to shake Mr. Malloy's hand. Wouldn't that be something? Even though he'd had to leave school to work and support Pa, Nathan would be better than the other kids because he'd know Collin Malloy.

Nathan pried open the leather-covered box. Inside, nestled against a bed of dark-blue velvet, the pocket watch sparkled. Prisms of sunlight shimmered on hundreds of tiny diamonds. Nathan gasped. Wow, it sure was pretty. It was probably worth a lot of money. Just one of them diamonds would set Pa up at that sanitarium. Nathan ran a finger along the gold watch case, his fingertip snagging on the hundreds of little gold clasps that held the jewels in place.

"Nat!"

Nathan snapped the box shut with one hand and shrank into the building's midmorning shadows. He tugged his newsboy cap down over his eyebrows. A fellow had to watch himself, especially when he was delivering something worth as much as this watch.

"Nat!"

The same voice, louder and more insistent, echoed against the walls. Nathan craned his neck around the corner of the building and came face-to-face with the local train engineer, Mr. Fitzgerald.

"Gee, Mr. Fitz! Whatcha hollerin' like that for?" Nathan tucked the box closer against his body. "You 'most scared me to death!"

He could talk like that to Mr. Fitzgerald, because the old man was a good sort. He often ran errands around the rail yard, and Mr. Fitzgerald let him sit in Big Engine No. 2, the locomotive he ran to and from Denver.

"Look here, boy. Do you still have the watch?" The engineer was panting, and his face was pale, like he'd seen a ghost.

"I still got it." Nathan held out the leather box. "Why?"

Mr. Fitz shoved Nathan's arm back against his side. "Don't go flashing it about, Nat. This is serious. You've got to take that box and hide it."

Nathan straightened. "No sir! I got to deliver this straightaway to the opera house. They're waiting on it. They're gonna give it to Mr. Malloy after he sings tonight."

"Mr. Malloy isn't gonna sing tonight, and you can't deliver that box. Listen, you've got to trust me on this. Take that box and hide it in No. 2, and then you go lie low for a couple of days." Mr. Fitz kept looking over his shoulder, like he was being chased by someone.

Nathan fought a rising tide of panic. Why was Mr. Fitz acting so strangely? And asking him to hide a valuable watch like that? Nathan had never missed a delivery, not in the two years he'd been working. It was quite a thing for a nine-year-old kid to be trusted to carry stuff back and forth, and if he didn't make this drop, then...

"Mr. Fitz, they're gonna think I'm a thief!"

"I'll take care of that. Don't worry." Mr. Fitz shoved two bits into his palm. "Just trust me. Go hide the box, and then go hide yourself. There are bad men after Malloy. Gangsters."

"Gee!" Gangster movies were the best ones to watch. "Do they have tommy guns?" Forget shaking hands with Mr. Malloy. He could see a real live gangster if he stuck around.

"Go on!" Mr. Fitz gave him a shove that sent him slipping down the pavement, his battered leather soles scraping along with a nails-on-chalkboard sound. "Do as I say, boy! And then get yourself out of town for a couple of days."

Nathan trotted obediently down the sidewalk, tucking the leather box further into his pants pocket. As he rounded the corner, he looked back. Mr. Fitz disappeared around the corner of the opera house. He must be headed toward the back entrance, where the dressing rooms were.

Squealing tires split the quiet stillness of the morning. Nathan dove back into the shadows. He didn't recognize the car, and no one around here drove like that. It must be the gangsters. His mouth went dry. All of a sudden, meeting one of them didn't seem so exciting.

Nathan took off running in the direction of the train yard. Behind him, one of the car doors opened and slammed shut.

"Hey, kid!"

The blood began pounding in Nathan's ears. Sounds of scuffling and shouting trailed him, but he wouldn't look back.

He was running like his life depended on it. Because this time, it just might.

1

Sadie Speers smiled encouragement as Mayor Edwin Marshall rose to address the group gathered around him. They were the very first passengers on the newly formed Silver Peak Scenic Railway. Just as he opened his mouth to speak, the train's whistle gave a short, shrill blast, and everyone laughed.

Edwin leaned forward slightly and grasped the padded mohair seats on either side of the aisle for support as the train chugged through the mountains, and he began again.

"I'd like to thank you all for coming this evening," he said. "When the Mountain Crest Railroad closed in the 1940s, no one knew for certain if this magnificent engine would ever run again. Tonight, we are pleased to welcome the Silver Peak Scenic Railway as part of our town's flourishing tourist industry."

Sadie added her applause to the rest of the passengers in the packed railroad car, clapping her kid-gloved hands until Edwin waved for silence. Her heart surged with pride. She and Edwin grew up together and dated in high school, but then life took them in different directions. After the passing of both of their spouses, however, they had found their way to each other once more, and in Edwin's company, Sadie was content. He looked so debonair tonight in his tuxedo, more at home in 1930s attire than in the casual outfits she encouraged him to wear throughout the week as the mayor of a thriving mountain community.

"As you know," Edwin continued, his dignified baritone voice ringing through the train car, "this 'maiden voyage' begins a week of festivities centered on Silver Peak history in the 1930s, when the Mountain Crest Railroad was in its prime. We have old-fashioned games planned for the children, a gospel music concert, and a film festival with a special tribute planned for Collin Malloy, the famous opera star turned Hollywood star."

Sadie smiled at the mention of Collin Malloy. When the investors in the Silver Peak Scenic Railway had approached the Historical Preservation Committee for festival ideas, Sadie had spent hours brainstorming with Edwin, trying to come up with events that would reflect the town's heritage throughout the Great Depression. It was her idea to pay tribute to Collin Malloy, who, while not a native of Silver Peak, had gotten his start as a performer at their opera house. Collin had been a particular favorite of Sadie's mother, and what better way to rekindle the glamour of that era than to pay homage to Silver Peak's most successful adopted son?

Edwin's steel-blue eyes twinkled in her direction for a moment before he turned his attention back to the passengers. "I'd like to say more, but the conductor would like to give everyone one last chance to sample the refreshments before we arrive back at the station. So if you want to hear more about a little surprise I have planned, linger for a few moments after we depart the train. I'll give you all the details before we head over to the Depot for the reception."

Sadie applauded with the crowd once more, her curiosity piqued. What surprise had Edwin planned for this week? She thought she knew all the events of the Railway Festival, from this inaugural train ride to the film festival.

She couldn't suppress a grin as she gazed at her reflection in the window beside her, which showcased a dusky Colorado sky. Her salt-and-pepper hair, normally styled for minimal maintenance, had been coaxed by her daughter, Alice, into marcel waves. Her hairstyle, crushed velvet gown, and lace stole made Sadie feel as though she'd stepped out of another time.

As she glanced around the railway car, she recognized several familiar faces even though everyone was dressed in period costume. Her best friend, Rosalind, whom everyone called Roz, sat just behind and across the aisle from her. Somehow, Roz's normal Bohemian style melded perfectly with 1930s glamour, and, along with a vintage pair of tortoiseshell glasses with sparkling touches of rhinestone around the lenses, she sported a turban with an ostrich feather as naturally as her straw gardening hat.

Across the car and up a few rows, Spike Harris looked more dapper than she'd ever seen him, wearing a tuxedo, his long hair slicked back. Spike usually wore a leather jacket and jeans, which felt natural for a musician and the owner of the Silver Peak Music Emporium, but tonight he could've been an extra in a Hollywood film.

She caught glimpses of other familiar faces here and there—Pastor Don Sweeting and his wife, Jeanne, who sported chandelier earrings so dazzling that light glinted off the prisms, and Roz's husband, Roscoe, owner of the town's hardware store, looking slightly upholstered and uncomfortable in a subdued suit.

But it was also heartening to see so many new faces in the crowd. Silver Peak was a small town and Sadie had lived here all her life, so she knew practically every member of their community. Just about everyone in town supported and encouraged both the historical preservation of the town and the development of the tourist trade so vital for its survival. Seeing so many familiar faces here tonight was to be expected, but many tourists had shown up as well, and all of them in costume.

She glanced around the car and caught the eye of Roz, who gave her an enthusiastic thumbs-up. By any measure, this event was a success. Purely in terms of the number of visitors it brought to Silver Peak, it had already accomplished its goal, since the whole purpose of the railway was to attract tourists from the neighboring ski resorts.

She glanced at the man sitting beside her in the aisle seat. The train seats had been assigned as tickets were bought, and as result, a nice mix of locals and tourists mingled together.

Like everyone else in the car, her neighbor was dressed elegantly in a period-appropriate tuxedo, but he kept his top hat on, tugged tightly over his head, his dark hair curling out from under the brim. He was in his forties, she guessed, and had a thick, full beard and a magnificent mustache. Sadie couldn't help thinking he looked like a cross between a mountain man and a Civil War general. While the effect was undercut somewhat by a pair of brown plastic-framed glasses with thick lenses, his piercing blue eyes were striking.

Sadie had tried to engage him in conversation early in the trip, but he had politely sidestepped all her comments and questions. She'd given up after ten minutes and knew no more about him now than she had when he'd sat down. He hadn't even told her his name.

As Sadie peeked at the stranger again, a vivacious brunette wearing a vintage uniform wheeled a cart up the aisle. She paused at each row, offering steaming cups of hot chocolate to the passengers. Sadie had met her during the planning for the train's first ride. Her name was Darcy Burke, and, like a few other part-timers on the train's staff, she was from a neighboring town. She also happened to be the niece of Jack Fitzgerald, the train engineer, and she shared her uncle's enthusiasm for the antique train.

As Darcy approached, the man sitting beside Sadie turned to her. "Would you like something?"

"Yes, I would. Thanks." Sadie smiled at him.

"Two, please." The man took the cups Darcy offered and looked at them in surprise. "Well, this is a luxury. Real china, just like in the old days."

"Oh yes." Darcy smiled at him. "Thanks to Mrs. Speers here, we have all the authentic things we need, right down to the chocolate mugs."

Sadie gratefully accepted her cup from her seatmate and grinned at the young woman. "The Antique Mine is always happy to lend a helping hand—or in this case, a few antiques. Are you enjoying your work here, Darcy?"

"I am. Being around all these antiques sure makes it beautiful." Darcy peeked into the silver plate chocolate pot. As she lifted its lid, her elbow knocked one of the ceramic mugs off the cart. It bounced off the cart's wheel and then shattered into a dozen pieces on the floor of the train.

Sadie felt her heart wrench at the sound and the sight of one of her beautiful Fire-King mugs destroyed. Passengers all around gasped, and Darcy cried out and crouched down, her shaking fingers clumsily picking up shards of mug.

"I'm so sorry!" she said, her voice high and shrill. "Oh, your beautiful mug! I'm so, so sorry, Mrs. Speers! I can't believe I did that!"

Sadie's neighbor slid out of his seat and helped Darcy pick the final pieces off the floor.

Sadie watched them in dismay for a moment before shaking herself out of it. It was just one mug, after all, and Darcy was near tears.

"It's okay, it's okay," she said, trying to soothe the young woman. "Worse things have happened. You haven't done any serious harm."

Darcy dumped the pieces of mug onto a lower shelf of the cart and nodded jerkily at Sadie's neighbor, who resumed his seat. "I don't know how to apologize enough, Mrs. Speers. You can ask Uncle Jack to take it out of my paycheck. It's only fair." She took a deep breath and seemed to gather herself. When she opened her eyes again, she fixed them with a shaky smile. "There'll be a table set up as you get off the train. Just set your cups down, and we'll take them to be washed." Darcy shot a nervous glance in Sadie's direction. "I promise to take good care of them. Truly. But if you'd rather someone else took them to wash, I'd understand."

"I'm not too worried, Darcy. They're Fire-King mugs. They're built to last." She looked at the pieces lying on the lower shelf of the cart and fought a smile. Well, maybe not *that* one. "This is just a fluke, I promise."

Most antiques were meant to be used, Sadie believed, which was why she'd lent the mugs and chocolate services to the train station for this event. Putting a beautiful object behind glass and never letting anyone use it again—what a waste! Obviously some artifacts were too fragile to withstand everyday wear and tear, but most antiques were more practical than people thought.

With a small wave, Darcy moved the cart up the aisle, stopping to chat here and there with other passengers. Sadie could see her slowly regain her equilibrium.

The man beside Sadie offered a charming smile. "You must own an antique store. What a great job."

"Yes—" Sadie began, but a shrill whistle rent the air.

Thundering groans rose from the many wheels and gears and machinery beneath them, and the train's momentum slowed.

Sadie looked around. A man across the aisle just behind her held his phone to his ear. "I can't hear you," he hollered. "Just a second." He rose, moving into the aisle. Beside him, a woman dressed in silver lamé clutched at her fox fur stole and began to follow him.

Darcy waved her arms from the back of the train. "Sir, please sit down. We'll be in the station in moments."

The woman in silver lamé tugged at the man's sleeve, and with a disgusted grunt he sat back down, running his hand through his dark hair. "Ridiculous. Can't even get a clear signal," he announced to the car in general.

The train shuddered to a stop with a final *whoosh* of the brakes. Sadie settled back into her chair with a happy sigh. Now that the ride was over she could join Edwin, who had been seated at a place of honor as the mayor so he could easily address the group, and find out what surprise he had in store for the town.

Turning toward the window, she noticed the brass tag screwed into the mahogany wall next to her. It read "13C" in Art Deco lettering. How perfect. She ran her fingertip along the tiny brass plaque. Every detail of the train had been preserved or restored back to its 1930s glory, when it had so briefly been the main transportation between Silver Peak and Denver.

Beside her, her seatmate stood to exit the train, but the aisle was full of passengers. Neither he nor Sadie was going anywhere for a few minutes.

Sadie began gathering her things to leave. She tried to arrange her lace shawl about her shoulders, but a corner of the fabric had gotten shoved down between the seat cushions and was caught on something. She gave a gentle tug, a gesture borne of many years of working with delicate fabrics, and pulled the shawl free. But it was heavy, tangled with something that glittered.

She unwound the fabric and smothered a gasp as the soft light from the light above revealed her find. A million prisms sparkled off the surface of a gentleman's pavé diamond pocket watch.

Sadie straightened and held the pocket watch out in the palm of her hand. Her antique-expert mind took over, and she examined the watch to see if it was authentic. She angled it carefully so the prisms would catch the light. The sparkles were so bright they hurt her eyes. It certainly passed the brilliance test. Would it stand up to a fog test? She held the watch up to her lips and breathed on it, a trick she'd learned while scouting antique jewelry. Real diamonds didn't fog up; fake ones, even very well done fakes, always did.

These diamonds didn't fog.

Who would leave a treasure like this on a train? This was no mere prop or costume piece that had fallen from one of the train staff's pockets. Someone must have lost it.

"What a stunning watch." The stranger beside her ducked back into his seat, peering intently at her hand. "Is it yours?"

"No. It must have been dropped by someone else." She clasped her hand around the watch. "I should notify the staff." Someone, somewhere would be missing this watch.

"Of course. Here, I'll get out of your way." With one fluid gesture, the man moved out of his seat and into the aisle, holding back the exiting passengers so that Sadie could slip out of her seat.

As Sadie stepped into the aisle, all the lights on the train went out. A wave of gasps and muffled exclamations swept through the car. Her shin hit something in the sudden blackness and she fell to her knees.

"Here." From the shadows, a hand grasped Sadie's gloved wrist. "Let me help you," her seatmate murmured in her ear. She was lifted back to her feet with a single graceful pull.

A few seconds later, the lights in the car flickered back on.

"Sorry about that, folks!" Darcy shouted from the back of the train car. "Everything's fine! Please continue exiting the train."

Sadie turned to thank the man who had come to her aid, but he was gone. Behind her, a column of passengers stood, all of them impatient to press onward. Where had the man who was sitting next to her gone? He couldn't just vanish into that crowd of jostling passengers.

"*Excuse me.*" The woman in the silver lamé gown pushed forward, eyeing Sadie as if she were the sole person in her way. "I'd like to get off this train, if you don't mind."

"Yeah. I'd like to return that call sometime this century." Her companion, tall and dark, rolled his brown eyes and sighed in exasperation.

"Oh, sorry. Of course." Sadie turned and started walking up the aisle. Then she paused and looked down at her empty hand.

The dazzling pocket watch was gone.

2

By the time Sadie had searched the floor around her seat for the watch, unsuccessfully, and made her way off the train, a small crowd had already gathered around Edwin. She rubbed her shin. Whatever she'd stumbled against was sure to leave a bruise on her leg.

She shook her head, her mind still reeling. In the space of just a few moments, perhaps even seconds, she'd found an invaluable pocket watch and then lost it, along with a fellow passenger she'd never seen before. The carnival atmosphere of the train party along with the sight of her fellow townspeople in period dress seemed surreal. Had she really held that watch after all? Had she really met that man? She knew her mind wasn't playing tricks on her, but it was hard to stay grounded in reality on a night like this.

She limped over to join the crowd that had gathered around Edwin. No need to call the conductor to report a crime that might or might not have happened, and that might or might not even be a crime. After all, perhaps the watch belonged to someone on the train, and he or she had picked it up when Sadie dropped it. She didn't even know what the situation *was* at this point. She would just have to wait and ask for Edwin's thoughts on the matter after he'd given his speech. As a former circuit court judge, Edwin had learned to study the facts and draw conclusions from them, and by talking to him, she'd be able to figure out what to do next—if anything even needed to be done.

Spike stood next to her, his arms wrapped across his chest as he rocked slowly back and forth in the cold.

"Spike, where's your coat?" Sadie chided him. "It's freezing out here!"

"All I had was my leather jacket." Spike smiled a little, looking down at the ground. "It looked funny with my tux."

Sadie laughed, and then turned her attention back to Edwin. He raised his hands, and silence descended over the group.

"I mentioned earlier that we're honoring Collin Malloy in a film tribute later this week," Edwin said, his breath coming out in puffs on the frosty evening air. "But what I didn't tell you is that there's a mystery connected to Collin Malloy's time in Silver Peak. In May 1931, Silver Peak planned to present Mr. Malloy with a gift to commemorate his many performances at our opera house and to congratulate him as he moved on to Hollywood. They had a lovely diamond pocket watch made just for him."

Sadie's head snapped up and her heart quickened a bit.

"However, something happened that night. The watch never made it to Mr. Malloy. No one is quite sure what happened to it, and though it was worth a fortune, it vanished into thin air. Mr. Malloy went to Hollywood and never returned to Silver Peak. The loss of Mr. Malloy's watch caused a lot of disappointment in the community. Everyone had worked so hard to pull enough money together to make something special for their adopted son, and then it disappeared. So I am asking the question that's never been answered—what happened to that diamond pocket watch?"

Sadie swallowed. Could she really have held it in her hands just a few moments earlier?

"As part of the festivities this week, we're organizing a treasure hunt. Check your attics. Check your cellars. Comb your mountain cabins. Walk along the Paseo River with metal detectors. If we can find the watch, we'll put it on display in the new train station, a reminder of what our town can do when we all work together. It's a symbol of Silver Peak's heritage and our can-do spirit."

The crowd broke into applause. Sadie felt like a deflated balloon. It was almost impossible that the watch she'd held could be some other watch. There couldn't be multiple priceless watches lost in Silver Peak. It had to have been Collin Malloy's watch, and it was gone. Again.

"I know it's a long shot, finding that watch after all these years, so we're going to make it worth your while. The finder of the watch gets VIP season tickets with backstage passes for the opera house. The best seats in the house for every single show, plus a chance to meet the performers."

The crowd applauded again, this time with a few cheers thrown in. Edwin grinned.

"In addition to the treasure hunt, we're sponsoring an essay contest for the younger set, a mystery-writing contest. The writer who dreams up the most creative hiding place for the watch wins. It doesn't have to be long; five hundred words should do it. The winner of the essay contest gets his or her picture in the paper and a gift certificate for dinner at Sophia's."

The applause this time was more subdued, and Edwin laughed. "I know dinner is waiting at the Depot, and it's getting colder out here as the sun sets. Rules for the treasure hunt and the essay contest will be published in the *Silver Peak Sentinel*. I'll see you over at the Depot!"

As the crowd dispersed, chased to their cars by the cold weather and the promise of delicious food, Edwin offered Sadie his arm. She tucked her fingertips into the crook of his elbow and walked with him to his silver BMW sedan.

She waited until Edwin had helped her in, closed her door, climbed in himself, and started the car. She turned to him. "Edwin, you're not going to believe this, but I am just about positive I found that pocket watch tonight."

"What?" Edwin's patrician face, illuminated by the dashboard and the pale glow of the street lamps outside, reflected astonishment. "Not Collin Malloy's watch, surely."

"I think so. It was the strangest thing. My shawl was tangled up on something in my seat, and when I unraveled it, I was holding a pavé diamond pocket watch. And they were real diamonds."

He turned to give her an incredulous look. "Can I see it?"

"Well, that's the thing... I stood up to show it to the conductor, and then everything happened at once. When the lights went out, I stumbled and fell, and when they came back on, the watch was gone."

As she told Edwin about the watch's disappearance, some questions began to form in her mind. Had she really stumbled? Or had she tripped or been pushed? How had the watch disappeared from her hand? She didn't remember losing hold of it, and yet she never felt someone take it from her.

"Do you think it was stolen?" Edwin asked.

Sadie sighed and shrugged. "I was just thinking about that. When the lights came up, it was gone. I searched for it. I can't say for sure if it was stolen, though. I suppose I could have dropped it but— No, no. I didn't drop it. It was in my hand one moment and gone the next."

"So it was taken from you." Edwin sounded more and more concerned. "The question is, was it indeed Collin Malloy's pocket watch that you were holding? Or was it just an amazing coincidence?"

"If I'd known it was his watch, I would have *watched* myself better," Sadie said, trying to lighten Edwin's solemn expression.

He groaned, but the corner of his mouth twitched with a grin. It felt good to get a smile out of Edwin, even if it took a pretty terrible pun to do so.

"And if it wasn't his watch, well, honestly, I doubt there are many pavé diamond pocket watches hanging around in Silver Peak. I am as sure as I can be that the diamonds were real. The watch itself felt heavy, like a solid gold piece should feel. And it looked authentic to the period, from what I could tell. What's interesting is that the bow—that's the little ring up at the top for a chain—was stiff. It didn't flop back and forth like one that had been worn very much. Even the crown, which would've been used to wind the watch, was set with a tiny diamond." She sighed. "It had to be real."

"Well, maybe we should search the train."

"I agree. It's definitely possible that I dropped it, even if I don't remember doing so. I wasn't able to look very thoroughly tonight."

"And it's also possible that someone attempted to take it from you but dropped it while the lights were off." Edwin guided the car into the Depot's parking lot, slowing down as partygoers passed by in their dress costumes. He glanced over at her with a thoughtful expression. "I can't believe you found the watch, Sadie!"

"Found it—and then lost it again." She shook her head.

"Well, yes. But don't you see? Now we know it actually still exists. Before, it was mostly theoretical. Now we know it's out there."

"Well, we have to find it again first. I'm so sorry I lost it." She turned in her seat to face Edwin more fully. "How did you find out about it in the first place? I've done some reading on Collin Malloy, but I've never heard the story about the watch."

Edwin put the car in park. "After it disappeared, the story faded too, so I'm not surprised that you hadn't heard about it. I only uncovered the story as I was organizing this week's festivities, trying to find out more about Malloy. I decided to highlight it this week because, beyond the monetary value of the watch, it symbolizes Silver Peak's generous and positive spirit."

She smiled at Edwin. It was no wonder that she enjoyed being in his company. He understood and loved so much of what she loved too. Still, her heart felt heavy. She'd held the long-lost watch in her hand. How had she lost it again so quickly?

They walked, arm in arm, into the Depot, where Edwin helped her remove her shawl. Then he was immediately claimed by the town's sole reporter, Troy Haggarty, who wanted more details on the treasure hunt for the write-up in the *Silver Peak Sentinel*.

Sadie shook off her disappointment at the loss of the watch and smiled at friends standing in the buffet line. As she picked through the dinner rolls, Jeanne Sweeting, Pastor Don's wife, approached. Her long chandelier earrings sparkled against her lovely cocoa-colored skin.

"Hi there, Sadie. Have you tried the Brie yet?"

"I'm working my way over there." Sadie said. She glanced around the restaurant, taking in the sumptuous spread of food and then the large number of people eating and socializing, dressed in their period finery. Many of them had been on the train ride. Perhaps she should start looking for the watch by figuring out what had become of all the people who were sitting around her when it vanished. She turned back to Jeanne. "Did you happen to see the fellow I was sitting by tonight?"

"I did! That was quite a mustache, wasn't it?"

"Definitely from another era!" Sadie smiled. "I found something on the train, and I can't be sure if it belonged to him or not. Did you happen to see where he went? I was hoping he'd be here, but I don't see him."

Sadie offered Jeanne an empty plate from the buffet table. No need to go into the details about the watch. If she went around announcing that she'd found the pocket watch, it could ruin the treasure hunt and might even cast suspicion on her. For now, she'd keep the find to herself. And who knew? Perhaps someone would find it wherever it had gone after she'd lost it.

Jeanne took the plate with a smile. "Well, after we arrived at the station, I was at the back of the train, waiting for Don. He stopped to talk to the conductor. I think I saw your seatmate talking to one of the girls who was working on the train. But by then Don was coming my way, and I wasn't really paying any attention."

"I see." Sadie frowned. How could her seatmate have vanished from the train so quickly? Yet he was spotted hanging around the train after he'd disembarked. A man who'd just stolen a valuable watch would run away, surely. "Do you happen to know which employee he was talking to?"

"Well, it was so dim in the station, and I was focused on Don," Jeanne admitted. "It was a woman, though. She was carrying a big plastic tub. It looked heavy, because she kept shifting it in her arms. But when he reached for it, she wouldn't let him have it."

A young woman with a heavy plastic tub? That could be Darcy, and the tub could well have been holding her Fire-King mugs, on their way to be cleaned.

"Thanks, Jeanne. He disappeared so quickly, I'm just happy to know I wasn't sitting by a ghost the whole time." Sadie laughed. "Now, should we attack that Brie? I'm so hungry, my stomach is growling."

Jeanne chuckled and led the way to the big wheel of cheese. As Sadie spread some on her plate, she remembered something. She had a biography of Collin Malloy at home. She'd bought it when they started planning the events for this week but never had a chance to do much more than thumb through it when things were slow at the Antique Mine.

When she got home tonight, after she'd changed out of her crushed velvet and let Hank out one last time, she'd give that book a look. It might contain a description or even a photograph of the diamond pocket watch.

"C'mon, Hank," Sadie called to her golden retriever as he rooted around in the darkness. "Time for bed."

The biography of Collin Malloy weighted the pocket of her fuzzy bathrobe, pulling it off-kilter. Now that she was home and changed into her flannel pajamas, she could do a little rooting around herself.

Hank trotted obediently past her into the back door and then sat expectantly, wagging his tail.

Sadie chuckled. "You're expecting a treat, aren't you?"

Hank responded by peering intently at her and licking his chops.

"To be honest, I wouldn't mind one myself."

Hank's plume tail wagged eagerly. Sadie gave him a treat, then put together a plate of Nilla Wafers and a glass of warm milk. Normally she'd just drink one more cup of coffee, but she had quite a lot at the Depot and these soothing, homey treats were just the thing for a chilly night like this.

Hank followed her up the stairs and parked himself at the foot of the bed, facing the fireplace, which filled the room with toasty warmth. Everything was perfect for a good read.

She set her snack on the bedside table and gathered her pillows to make a comfortable pile at the head of the bed. Then she climbed in, reveling in the warmth of the flannel sheets. Her daughter, Alice, had given her this set about a month ago, and they were so cozy it was sometimes hard to get out of bed in the morning. At least Hank kept her active, she reflected, giving him an affectionate glance. He'd never let her sleep in.

She said her nightly prayer, thinking about what a blessing her home life was. How fortunate she was to still have her family's wonderful ranch house, to have friends like Edwin and Roz and the Sweetings in her life, and to have her daughter and grandchildren living so nearby. With a last "amen" of gratitude, she settled down under the covers and grabbed her book, which she'd set next to her snack.

Before she opened the book, she scrutinized the cover. The old saying "You can't judge a book by its cover" didn't apply to antique dealers. A book's cover could reveal quite a lot, as she'd learned over the years. It could divulge a book's age or indicate its condition.

This book was brand-new, its jacket shiny and crisp. An old sepia-tone photograph of Collin Malloy graced the cover. His hair was swept back from his handsome face, and he wore a fine suit. Her eyes fell on a pocket watch chain dangling discreetly from his pocket—but, of course, it wasn't the pocket watch the citizens of Silver Peak had intended to give him.

She traced her fingertips over the raised Art Deco lettering of the title. *Collin Malloy: A Hunger for Life*. Why was Malloy so hungry for life? Hadn't he lived and experienced more than most folks did in several generations? After all, he had achieved fame on an international level.

Sadie paged through the book slowly. There were dozens of photographs of Malloy interspersed with the text. A photo of him as a child exposed, more accurately than any words could, his hardscrabble Irish background: a scrawny, wiry barefoot boy in overalls, wearing one of those bowl haircuts thrifty mothers imposed upon their children. Later photos revealed the transformation of Malloy from reedy teenager to magnetic opera tenor. These photos also revealed Malloy's penchant for vibrant blondes, as a different smiling woman graced almost every shot.

She flipped back to the index and located the section on Malloy's ties to Silver Peak. It was far too brief for Sadie's taste—

after all, Silver Peak deserved its own chapter, in her opinion—but it still yielded valuable information.

Malloy held Silver Peak in high esteem for the length of his career, and spoke of the little mountain town with great respect in all his interviews with the press. The inhabitants of Silver Peak regarded Malloy as one of their own, despite his birth and upbringing in Denver's Irish slum. In fact, the town made plans to present Malloy with a fine diamond watch, which was announced in newspapers all across the state. However, it appears that the gift never was given, as Malloy missed his final concert in Silver Peak in his haste to attend a coveted screen test with International Pictures in Hollywood.

Sadie closed the book and placed it to one side. So Collin Malloy had never received the watch because he missed his last concert at the Silver Peak Opera House. But that still didn't explain why or how the watch had disappeared.

She felt more certain than ever that she had held Malloy's watch on the train. But what had happened to it? Was it still hidden in some cranny on the train, jolted out of her hand when she stumbled? Or had someone—someone like her mysterious seatmate—stolen it from her? How had it gotten on the recently refurbished train in the first place? One question led to another. Sadie was thankful she'd avoided that last cup of coffee, because it would be very hard indeed to fall asleep tonight with all these thoughts whirling around her mind.

Even though she had a full day of work ahead tomorrow, she decided she would make time to go back to the train to search for some answers. Maybe she would have better luck by daylight, without impatient passengers stepping around her in their haste to disembark.

3

"Hi, Sadie! I'm so sorry I'm late." Julie Pearson, Sadie's part-time employee, rushed into the Antique Mine, her long blonde hair swinging behind her. "Getting the boys set for hockey practice was a nightmare." She shed her jacket, a lovely 1960s-style mod peacoat, revealing an adorable cashmere twin set that she'd paired with a wool circle skirt.

"Don't worry. The shop's been pretty quiet this morning, especially for a Saturday. Maybe some of those tourists in town for the reopening of the railway will stop by."

Sadie cast an admiring glance at her stylish employee. Julie, even in the midst of her harried life as the wife of the town pediatrician and mother of two rambunctious boys, always looked as put together as a model in a *Vogue* editorial.

Julie stopped halfway into the shop. "Oh! You finished the display! It looks great."

Sadie followed her gaze. In honor of the week's festivities, she'd decided to create a display honoring Collin Malloy. She'd had a crate of old photos of classic Hollywood stars in her back room for ages, so she dug it out, did some research on Collin Malloy's film career and the other actors who had shared the silver screen with him, and pulled as many photos as she could find. Then she'd cleared a generous section of wall and hung all the photos in antique frames.

A blown-up portrait of Collin Malloy was in the center, with the other pictures hung in a cloud around him. Despite his short career—only two years—he'd worked with so many well-known stars. Clark Gable, Ginger Rogers, Fred Astaire, and Joan Crawford graced her wall in striking black-and-white portraits. Sadie's mother's favorite actress, Margaret Malone, was up there in mid-dance routine, as was an actress Sadie wasn't familiar with named Betty Bright. Sadie had almost left her out of the display, but she loved the candid on-set photo of the young blonde so much she included it after all.

"You think it's okay?" Sadie asked. Even without Julie's touch, she thought it looked pretty good. But she'd let her design-gifted employee adjust it if she wanted.

Julie eyed the display, finally pointing at the picture of Margaret Malone. "I might move her a couple inches to the left, for the balance, but otherwise I think it's perfect."

Sadie laughed and feigned exaggerated relief by wiping her hand across her forehead. Julie laughed and walked to the counter.

Sadie admired her outfit as she approached. "Where'd you find such a cute sweater set?"

"Online from a vintage shop. It makes me feel like Olivia Newton John in *Grease*."

"Yes, that's it exactly!" Sadie exclaimed. "Does that make your husband John Travolta?"

Julie's eyes lit up. "Oh, Chad will *hate* that. I can't wait to tell him." She flicked her long hair over her shoulder and assumed command of the cash register. "Okay, boss. I am in control now!"

Sadie laughed. "Well, as I'm clearly not needed here, I'm going to head over to the railway station and pick up some of the antiques we lent out for last night's party."

She was also going to look through the train and see if she could find the watch, but now was not the best time to get into that with Julie. Her employee hadn't been at the party last night, so she hadn't heard Edwin's speech and wouldn't have seen anything that might help Sadie's search. And Sadie still didn't think talking about the watch, even to Julie, made sense at this point.

"Are you sure you can handle all that? Those tubs of dishes are heavy."

"I'll be fine. Anything that doesn't fit in my Tahoe, I'll get help with. Maybe Edwin can help me out this afternoon." Sadie grabbed her keys from their spot on the counter and pulled on her cozy fleece North Face jacket. Julie loved to be fashionable, but Sadie preferred practicality and warmth. "Be back as soon as I can."

She started to head out the door but turned back.

Julie stood there, holding out Sadie's big brushed-aluminum travel mug, a mischievous smile lighting her face. "Forget something?"

"Yes! I wouldn't have gotten far without that." Julie knew Sadie couldn't do without her morning coffee. Or her afternoon coffee. Or her evening coffee. Sadie grabbed the mug gratefully. "See you later!"

Once she was carefully tucked into her Tahoe, the steaming mug filling the vehicle with the comforting smell of roasted coffee beans, she rolled down Main Street in the bright Colorado sunshine. As she drove, she let her love for Silver Peak fill her heart. Seeing all the familiar, unique shops lining the street, passing friends and neighbors who returned her smiles and waves, reminded her how blessed she was to live in such a vibrant, close-knit community.

When she pulled into the train station parking lot, she could see the engine parked on the tracks. "Engine No. 2" had been painted on its side. The paint had faded years ago, along with the old Mountain Crest logo. The new Silver Peak Scenic Railway logo, designed to complement the old advertising, was hand-painted beside the original marks in subdued colors.

What a fight that had been, one that Edwin had to step in and settle between the railway partners and the historic preservationists. The historians had wanted to leave everything the way it had looked in the thirties, while the railway folks had wanted to advertise and identify their trains. Edwin himself had approved the final compromise. Sadie suspected that it wouldn't be the last time Edwin's knack for mediating would come in handy.

The train's conductor, Jack Fitzgerald, hailed her as she approached. Sadie waved and smiled in return. Jack came from a long line of train enthusiasts; in fact, his grandfather had been the engineer on this train during the very era they were celebrating this week.

Sadie opened the station's main door and entered the waiting room. The station was newly built, since the old station had been converted to the Depot restaurant. The investors had built this new depot along the same blueprint as the original station, and it looked as authentic as if it had been in Silver Peak forever.

A handful of employees and volunteers in black sweatshirts bustled around, folding up chairs, tearing down streamers, and emptying trash cans. They smiled and waved at Sadie as she walked in.

She found Jack Fitzgerald in his office.

"Well, if it isn't the Antique Lady!" Jack pushed his cap back from his forehead and grinned. "Come to collect your things?"

"If you don't need them anymore, I'll take them back to the Antique Mine."

Jack shook his head. "You're too early. They haven't come back from the cleaner yet. We're expecting them this afternoon. Is that okay?"

Sadie smiled. "Of course. I can come back later, no problem." She paused. Maybe she could talk to Darcy. After all, Darcy had helped clean up last night. Perhaps she had seen the watch or could help Sadie look for it. And Sadie could ask about her mysterious seatmate, see if Darcy had indeed been the woman Jeanne had seen talking to him last night. "By the way, is your niece here? I wanted to make sure she wasn't still upset about breaking that mug last night. It was really no big deal."

"Darcy?" Jack frowned and shook his head. "Naw, Darcy's late today, which isn't like her. Usually she's pretty punctual. She was supposed to be here at nine to help with cleanup."

Sadie pushed back her coat sleeve and glanced at her watch. "Well, it's only a little past ten. Maybe she just overslept."

"Yeah, probably. Hey, what'd you think about the event? I mean, except for when we lost power. I nearly had a heart attack when that happened." As a retired teacher, Sadie couldn't help but think that Jack looked like an abashed little boy asking for approval on a less-than-perfect homework paper.

"It was great! The lights were only off for a few moments. Seconds, really. I don't think it ruined anyone's night." Except possibly her own. Sadie shrugged. "Do you know what caused the lights to go out?"

Jack shook his head. "I looked to see if there was some kind of mechanical fault, because I sure don't want it to become a regular thing, but everything was intact. We were just lucky it only lasted a few moments and no one got hurt."

Sadie didn't mention her shin. She didn't want Jack to feel bad. He clearly had enough on his mind.

A small crash erupted inside the station.

A volunteer ran into the office. "Mr. Fitz! We dropped one of the tables. I think it scuffed the floor."

"Oh boy," Jack said, then bade Sadie an apologetic good-bye.

Sadie walked back through the station, keeping an eye out for Darcy but not seeing her. Out in the parking lot, she climbed into her vehicle and took a long sip from her coffee mug. Then she backed out of her parking space and swung the Tahoe onto the main road.

As she was leaving, a small hatchback slowed to turn into the station's parking lot. Sadie glanced over at the driver.

It was Darcy.

Sadie gave her horn a tap and waved, but Darcy, after catching Sadie's eyes, ducked a little into her seat. Then, instead of turning into the parking lot, she accelerated and drove away.

Sadie pulled over and watched in her rearview mirror as Darcy continued down the street, away from the train station.

That was odd. Darcy had certainly seen her. So why had she left?

Sadie sat and sipped her coffee, her engine idling.

Well, odd behavior or not, she needed to get back to the shop. But she would definitely return to the train station later, when she might have a chance to speak with Darcy.

4

The parking space closest to the Antique Mine's door was taken up by a huge bright-yellow hybrid SUV. In fact, the SUV was taking up two parking spaces, straddling the white marker.

Sadie shrugged and parked in the next space over.

Sadie got out of the Tahoe and walked to the door of the shop. She couldn't help eyeing the space-hogging SUV as she rounded her car. Intentional rudeness was rare around these parts. Most everyone in Silver Peak was pretty polite, especially when it came to sharing personal space. She wondered if the SUV belonged to a tourist.

As Sadie entered the shop, she nearly ran into a man who was pacing back and forth at the front of the shop, muttering angrily. He gave her a hard glare over his shoulder as he brushed past her, and Sadie saw a Bluetooth phone device glowing in his ear.

"Look, I told you," he growled, turning away from Sadie. "We need to sell now. The shares are peaking, and we could save the whole thing."

Sadie recognized him as the impatient man who'd sat behind her on the train, the one who'd been frustrated that he couldn't get a signal on his phone.

She looked around. Julie was bent over the jewelry case with a customer. Contrary to her usual practice, she had placed several pieces of costume jewelry on the scrap of velvet they used to showcase pieces. Normally, Julie was very precise and only laid out one piece at a time. Not that they had that big of a problem with theft in Silver Peak, but still, caution was a virtue.

Julie looked up, giving Sadie a strained smile, and raised her eyes to the shop's pressed-tin ceiling with a little shake of her head. "Hi, Sadie. I can help with the boxes in a minute."

Before Sadie could reply, the customer waved her hand listlessly at Julie. "I don't like that one. Put it back. I can't abide turquoise, real or fake. But get out that little owl brooch. I want to see it up close."

Sadie recognized the woman as well, as she'd also been on the train. She'd traded her silver lamé dress for a fur coat, but it was the same woman who had asked Sadie to get out of her way after the lights in the train came back on.

"No problem." Julie tucked the offending jewelry back into the case. "Do you still want these others out?"

"Of course I do! Don't you see I am trying to make a decision?" The woman pulled her coat closer about her ears. "It's freezing in here. Don't you have a heater?"

"We do, and we also have a wonderful old woodstove," Julie said, sounding defensive.

Sadie decided it was time to step in and help out her assistant. "The high ceilings in these old buildings make it difficult to heat it as efficiently as a new building."

The woman pivoted on one booted heel and lowered her oversized sunglasses to give Sadie an assessing glare. "And who are you?"

Sadie joined Julie behind the jewelry counter and put out her hand for the woman to shake. "I'm Sadie Speers, proprietor of the Antique Mine. Welcome to Silver Peak. Are you in town for the train opening?"

"You're the owner?" The woman pushed her sunglasses up onto her head, perching them at her hairline.

"Guilty as charged," Sadie said with a smile. "I think I saw you on the train yesterday. I hope you're enjoying your stay in Silver Peak."

"Well, my husband and I were staying at a resort in Aspen, and this town sounded like a lark." She shrugged and pointed at the man who was still pacing at the front of the shop and muttering into his phone. "Anyway, I collect antique costume jewelry. I wanted to see if you had anything interesting."

"Well, you came to the right place." Sadie patted her assistant on the shoulder. "Why don't you take a break, Julie? I can help Mrs.—"

"Elliott. Grace Elliott." The customer folded her arms across her chest.

With a grateful nod and a surreptitious roll of her eyes, Julie retreated to the back room.

"I don't see much worthwhile here. You've got to understand that I'm a real collector." She sniffed. "You can't just pawn off any old Sarah Coventry piece on me. I want the real deal. Now, take this owl brooch, for example. This…" Grace picked up the brooch and held it up. "This could be something."

"It is, indeed," Sadie said. "It's a Hattie Carnegie original from 1938. I purchased it from an estate in Denver a while back. Isn't it lovely?"

Grace gave a little gasp and turned the piece over. Sadie bit her bottom lip to keep from breaking into a knowing grin. She'd managed to impress her customer, that much was certain. Grace Elliott might consider herself an aficionado, but she'd never get a good deal by letting on that she was excited like that.

"It *is* a Carnegie." Grace clasped her hand around the brooch and walked over to her husband. He continued to pace and carry on an agitated conversation. "Thomas, get off that phone. I need your credit card," she said as regally as if she were Marie Antoinette. "A real Carnegie," she added in an undertone that carried throughout the store.

Thomas waved his hand at her with a shushing gesture, but Grace would not be deterred. She stuck her hand in his back pocket and grabbed his wallet.

Thomas yelped and turned around. "Good grief, Grace. Can't you just wait until I'm done?" He scowled down at his wife.

"No, because you take too long and I want this now. If I waited until you were done with every phone conversation, I'd never get anything accomplished." She waved the black leather wallet under his nose. "And I'm buying this brooch."

"No, Grace. We can't—"

Grace turned her back on him and stalked back up to the counter. "You always say we can't afford the stuff I like, and then you go out and buy stuff you like." She turned briskly to Sadie. "Okay, how much?"

Sadie quoted her price, then sat back expectantly. Over the years she'd witnessed many husband and wife disagreements in many antique stores, including her own. She knew better than to get involved.

"Deal." With a flourish, Grace unfurled an accordion of credit cards from the wallet, encased in a plastic sleeve. She slid one out. "Put it on this one."

Sadie slid the card through the reader, but the machine emitted a baleful bleat. Rejected. She sighed deeply. This was not going to be pleasant.

"I'm so sorry, Mrs. Elliot, but the machine doesn't seem to like this card."

"Try it again," Grace said. She had shucked her fur coat and was pinning the brooch onto her cowl-necked mohair sweater.

Sadie obliged. The card reader beeped again.

"I'm afraid this one just won't go through. Do you have another?" Sadie eyed the wallet. Would Grace have to go through every single card before they found one that worked?

"Here." Thomas strode to the counter, grabbed his wallet back from his wife, and shuffled out a stack of cash. "Will this do?"

"Of course." Sadie gave him a grateful smile. "Thank you."

"Good. C'mon, Grace."

Grace was busy trying to arrange her fur coat so the brooch showed. "Fine," she muttered. "I'm going to wear this all week."

"You're planning to stay for the rest of the festival?" Sadie gave them both a warm smile. They were out-of-town tourists, after all, the kind of people Silver Peak depended on for much of its business.

Thomas rolled his eyes. "I just came for the train ride. Grace is the one who wanted to stay for the whole enchilada."

"We're certainly glad you came. If you want a good cup of coffee, stop next door at Arbuckle's. They've got the best joe in town. Oh, and the best cinnamon rolls too!"

"Yes, we know." Grace waved her hand dismissively. "Jane at the B and B told us already."

"Did you enjoy the train ride?"

"It was fine. C'mon, Grace! Let's go." Thomas turned away, than activated his Bluetooth earpiece and began muttering again as he approached the front door. Grace trailed after him, settling her sunglasses on the bridge of her nose.

Well, that was too bad. Sadie had hoped she could ask Grace more about their experience on the train, but they certainly didn't seem inclined to chat.

The moment the door banged shut behind them and jangled the chime above the door, Julie poked her head around one of the china cupboards. "Oh, thank goodness. I thought they'd never leave."

Sadie laughed. "They *are* bringing business into town, though. I've had that Carnegie piece for months—never thought I'd sell it. In fact, I was getting ready to sell it on eBay."

Julie moved toward the jewelry case and froze. "Wait a minute. I thought I had the poinsettia brooch out too." She bent and inspected the jewelry case. "It's not in there, Sadie. That poinsettia is missing."

5

"Are you sure you took it out?"

Sadie moved closer and peered into the case. Sure enough, the poinsettia brooch was not in its usual spot, next to a collection of vintage Christmas tree pins.

"I'm certain I did. She made fun of it after I brought it out and said she'd never pay retail prices for pot metal." Julie straightened, her face draining of color. "Oh, Sadie. You don't think she stole it, do you?"

Sadie shook her head. "It's hard to imagine Mrs. Elliott would drop three hundred dollars on a Carnegie piece only to swipe a twenty-dollar novelty pin."

"Well, either way, I'll pay for it." Julie wrung her hands together. "I've got a twenty in my purse. Let me go get it."

"No, don't." Sadie reached across the counter and laid her hands on Julie's shoulders. "It'll turn up. I'm not worried about it, okay? And anyway, I know where you live."

Julie let out a relieved laugh. "True! Or you could always dock my paycheck." Her sunny smile returned. "At my wages, that could take a while."

Sadie laughed. "It'll be fine. I'm sure it'll turn up."

The phone rang, and Julie answered it. "Antique Mine, may I help you? Oh!" She held out the phone. "Sadie, it's Alice."

Normally Alice helped out at the Antique Mine on Saturdays and usually brought her children, Theo and Sara, along unless it was their father's turn to take them. This weekend, though, she'd said she'd be unavailable.

Alice got along fine with her ex-husband, Cliff, and they shared the duties of raising their children without stress or drama. But that arrangement could never equal being married and sharing the happy times and hard times together. Cliff had a thriving dental practice in Denver and was a pleasant and helpful ex-husband. But Sadie often wished he and Alice would somehow reconcile. Alice refused to talk about the possibility, however, and Sadie didn't push her.

Sadie accepted the phone. "Hi, Alice."

"Hey, Mom, did you get my text?" Alice's voice, normally so placid and even, sounded full of something, like she had a secret.

Sadie felt her pockets idly for her cell phone. "No, actually, I must've left my phone in the car. What's up?"

"Well, I thought you'd get a kick out of this... I have a date."

Sadie blinked. "Really? With who? Where did you meet him?"

Alice laughed. "Goodness, Mom, you'd think I'd never been on a date before." Her voice grew more thoughtful. "Though I guess I haven't dated anyone seriously since Cliff and I broke up, so it has been a while."

"Don't worry, it'll be fun," Sadie said. "Now tell me about him! What's his name? How did you meet?"

Alice hesitated. "I haven't actually met him in person yet. Just online."

"Online dating?" Sadie felt her smile widen and she couldn't resist the urge to tease her daughter. "Maybe I should read his profile."

"Mom!"

"Sorry. So it's a blind date?"

"Yes and no. I mean, I know what he looks like and we've exchanged quite a few e-mails. He seems like a nice person, so I thought…" Her voice trailed off. "Oh, Mom. I don't know what I thought. I feel so ridiculous. I haven't dated anyone in years."

"Well, don't fret." Sadie adopted the same brisk, cheerful tone she used whenever Alice began the process of what they called "doomsday thinking" as a child. "Remember that song you used to sing in Sunday school? 'The devil is a sly old fox. If I could catch him I'd put him in a box.' The devil loves it when you feel down on yourself."

Alice laughed. "Oh, Mom. Now you sound ridiculous."

"So what's his name?" Sadie twisted the phone cord around her finger. Somehow, it felt right to be having this conversation on an old-fashioned telephone. Talking about boys required fidgeting, and you couldn't do that on a cell phone.

"Arthur. Arthur Reed. He's an insurance broker in Denver. We're going to the country-and-western dance here on Friday night. Cliff will have the kids, and Arthur wants to see Silver Peak."

"Well, I look forward to meeting him. If he wants to see Silver Peak, then I like him already."

The chime above the door sounded as Edwin ducked in. Sadie smiled and waved.

"Edwin's here," she said. "I'm going to trick him into helping me load up a few things at the train station."

"Tell him I said hi. I hope the party last night was fun. I wish I could've gone, but I can't miss Theo's basketball practice."

"It was wonderful, and the train is already a tourist attraction. Tell Theo and Sara there's a treasure hunt and an essay contest. I'll fill you in on the details as soon as I can." Sadie slowly unknotted the telephone cord. "I'll talk to you later, okay?"

"Will do, Mom. Thanks for not allowing me to freak out. Love you."

"Love you too, dear." Sadie hung up and turned to Edwin. "Hello, stranger! Showing your face here today was a bad idea. You do know I am about to put you to work, don't you?"

"Yes, I suspected as much. So I brought energy food." Edwin pointed to a stack of Styrofoam containers he had placed neatly on the counter. "Lunch for you, me, and Julie. Takeout from Los Pollitos."

At the sound of her name, Julie reappeared from the back room. She clapped her hands at the sight of the food. "Yay! But I need to give you a piece of my mind, Edwin. My boys have dug up part of our yard looking for Collin Malloy's watch. They say they're seeking buried treasure for the treasure hunt." She grinned. "But I forgive you. You've won me over with food. My stomach was starting to growl. A girl works up an appetite dealing with people like the Elliotts."

"The Elliotts?" Edwin's wiry brows rose inquisitively as he handed Julie one of the boxes and a plastic-wrapped set of utensils. "New people in town?"

"Oh, just some high-maintenance customers." Julie accepted the box gratefully. "Mmm. I smell enchiladas."

"I got enchiladas and tacos for us all, since I couldn't choose between them." Edwin offered a box to Sadie with a grin.

They crowded around the counter and perched on stools. Sadie fell silent for a moment, mulling over her conversation with Alice. She was proud of Alice for being brave enough to try to find someone to spend her life with. Sadie glanced over at Edwin. She knew all too well how awkward it was to enter the dating world again, even with someone you'd known for years.

"Alice has a date," Sadie said without quite meaning to.

"That's awesome!" Julie beamed. "Good for her."

"How did she meet him?" Edwin's expression was more guarded than Julie's. "Do we know him?"

Sadie suppressed a grin. Was Edwin feeling a little paternal toward her daughter? That was nice, actually. It felt good to have someone who shared a little of the feeling of responsibility she carried.

"That's just it. She's never met him before. They've been chatting online."

"*Hmm.*" Edwin's eyebrows drew together and he shook his head. "I don't know how I feel about that."

"A lot of people find dates online," Julie said reassuringly. "It's hard to meet new guys these days. One of my friends from college was divorced, and she found her second husband through an online dating site. He's a great guy, and they're really happy. So you never know."

"I admit it seems a little odd to me, but I don't have anything against it." Sadie scooped up a bite of her enchilada with her fork. "I'm happy Alice is dating again. I want her to find someone to share her life with. It's just hard for me to imagine wanting to date someone based on a few e-mail exchanges." She laughed. "But then, it's probably hard for Theo and Sara to imagine writing actual letters to a penpal."

"Times are changing," Julie remarked with a shrug. "The world is both growing and shrinking."

"Well, in any case, we'll all have a chance to meet Arthur this weekend." Sadie closed her to-go box. "He's meeting her at the dance Friday night."

"Good. I'm sure he's a great guy." Edwin eyed her closed to-go box. "Is that my signal? Are you ready to put me to work?"

Sadie laughed. "Only if you're done. I don't want to rush you, especially since you brought Los Pollitos to us."

"Yeah, thanks for lunch, Edwin." Julie smiled. "I feel so much better. I could take on a whole store full of Elliotts now."

"I want to hear all about this couple," Edwin said as he closed his box. "Am I going to get the full rundown in the car?"

"Oh yes. Don't worry about *that*. Worry about how many heavy boxes I'm about to make you carry." Sadie grabbed her purse from behind the register and dug out the keys to her Tahoe. "Ready?"

Jack opened the door to the office and ushered Sadie and Edwin inside. He gestured toward a stack of boxes and tubs in one corner. "You're right on time. They just arrived fifteen minutes ago."

Sadie eyed the pile and frowned. "Is this all of it? There were three tubs of mugs, cups, and saucers, and two boxes—one for the silver coffee service, and one for the silver hot chocolate set." She peeked inside each tub. "This is most of my cups and saucers, and the coffee service. The Fire-King mugs and chocolate set aren't here."

Jack looked at the two tubs and one box in the corner of his office and his face fell. "You're right. This is only half of it. Let me go check with a couple of people, see if I can track down the rest."

"Sure, no problem."

While they waited, Sadie and Edwin each carried one of the tubs out to her Tahoe, and her bruised shin began to ache. When she returned to Jack's office, he was back, and he didn't look happy.

"Sadie, I am so sorry to tell you this, but I think we're missing a couple of your things." Jack Fitzgerald frowned as he consulted his clipboard. "I thought maybe the other two boxes were put somewhere else by mistake, but my staff swears this is all that came back from the cleaners."

Edwin hefted the last tub from the office and headed for the Tahoe. Sadie turned to Jack. "Maybe they're still being cleaned. Maybe they just sent over the first batch."

"Maybe, but they didn't say anything like that when they delivered these. They acted like we were all finished." Jack glanced at her, a worried frown settling over his expression. "It's so strange that only some of it is missing."

"*Hmm.* Well, let's hope they'll turn up. Maybe someone just put them in the wrong pile during all the cleanup after the party."

"Maybe," Jack said, offering them a look of apology. "I'll look into it some more."

The Fire-King mugs and the hot chocolate service were only worth about two hundred to three hundred dollars altogether—not a huge portion of her inventory—but she would prefer to have them back. She had known there was some risk that her antiques could be lost or damaged when she lent them to the station, though.

"Did Darcy ever make it in today?" Sadie asked. "I'd still love to speak to her."

"Well, no." Jack studied Sadie for a moment, and he seemed to be trying to make a decision. "I don't think she'll be coming in, actually." He paused again, then gave a sad shrug. "She quit."

Darcy quit? Sadie's heart sank. "Oh no! I'm sorry, Jack. Do you know where she lives? I'd like to send her a thank-you note for all her good work."

Jack shook his head. "My brother and his family live out west, in Crater Lake. I just don't get why she'd quit like this without at least talking to me first. Especially right before her wedding. I thought she liked this job." Jack glanced at the clock on his office wall. "I've got a meeting in about ten minutes, Sadie. I'd better go get cleaned up. But I'll let Darcy know you appreciated her work, and I'll stay on the lookout for those missing pieces. If we can't find them, we'll pay you for them."

Sadie nodded. "Thank you, Jack. I'm sure you'll find them. Do you mind if I climb aboard one last time?"

"Be my guest." Jack gave her a harried smile. "Who knows? Maybe your mugs are still in there."

"Thanks, Jack. By the way, you don't happen to have a copy of the seating chart I could have, do you? You know, as a souvenir." She wanted to be sure who was sitting near her when she found the watch—and when it disappeared again.

"Um, yeah, I guess that would be okay, since the event's over." He pulled a document out of his desk drawer. "We didn't have a formal manifest, but this should give you an idea of where everyone was sitting."

Sadie accepted the photocopied document and unrolled it. Names were scrawled in pencil across each box delineating a seat.

"Thanks, Jack. Enjoy your meeting!" Sadie smiled and waved as she left the office. As she walked out of the station, Edwin was strolling up the sidewalk. "Want to take another look at the train?" she asked him.

"Absolutely." Edwin gave her an assessing look. "Are we looking for the missing watch?"

Sadie nodded. "I want to make sure the watch isn't still on the train, but I also want to get a better sense of who was sitting around me last night." She grasped the wrought-iron banister as she made her way up the stairs into the train car. "I don't think we're going to find the watch, though. I feel pretty certain it was taken right out of my hand."

"So who could have taken it?"

"I've been wondering the same thing." She thought about Darcy. The young woman seemed to have run off when she last saw Sadie, so she might have been the woman Jeanne Sweeting saw with the mystery man last night, and she'd quit today. "I hate to say it, but the young woman who was working on the train yesterday, Darcy Burke, is at the top of my list." Sadie explained what Jack had told her about his niece.

"*Hmm.*" Edwin began pacing down the length of the train, pausing to examine each seat, sliding his hand between the cushions. "How do you think she might have taken it?"

"I'm not exactly sure. But who else had better access to the train and all the stuff going on behind the scenes?" Sadie bent down to look underneath a padded mohair seat. "Maybe someone knew that the watch was on the train. Who better to get on board and track it down than someone working here?"

"True, but if Darcy knew the watch was on the train, why didn't she just take it before the event started?"

"Great question," Sadie said, moving to the next row of seat cushions. "I'm not sure. I also can't help but think about the man sitting next to me. He saw me with the watch, and then, when the lights went out, he disappeared. Of course, go figure, I never learned his name."

"Well, let's take a look at the seating chart."

Sadie wiggled out from under a row of seats and handed it to him.

Edwin unfolded it. "So the man sitting beside you was named..." He paused. "Sadie, no one is listed for that seat."

"Are you sure?"

Sadie peeped over his shoulder. Sure enough, the seat next to her was left blank. Yet every other seat on the train had a name scrawled across it. The Elliotts occupied the places just behind and across the aisle from hers. Spike was up closer to the front. Edwin held the place of honor in the first row. But the seat beside her was blank.

"But there was a man there," she insisted. "He had dark hair, and bright blue eyes." She was starting to feel crazy. "He even helped me when I fell. At least, I think he did."

"Did anyone else see him?" Edwin asked.

"Yes, actually. Thankfully, or I really would start to think I'd imagined him. Jeanne Sweeting thinks she might have seen him talking to one of the staff after we arrived back at the station. And from her description, I feel pretty sure it was Darcy."

Sadie looked over the passenger list again. It resembled a sort of blueprint, showing the exits to the train, the lavatories, and the technical details of the train car. She folded it up again to take home so that she could refer to it if she needed it again.

"Well, you had the watch in your hand when the man helped you up," Edwin said. "He would be the most logical possibility as the one who took it."

"True." Sadie sat in one of the seats and mulled over the events of the previous night, trying to remember all the details. The more she thought about it, the more elaborate it seemed. "Still, I'm beginning to wonder if more than one person was involved in taking the watch. If it was some kind of small heist."

Edwin looked concerned but also a little amused. He sat beside her. "What makes you think that?"

"Well, I stumbled and fell just before I lost the watch." She rubbed her shin. "But it's possible I was purposely tripped. If I was, whoever did it must have been on my left side, and the man who helped me was on my right. In fact, he was holding my hand as I stumbled, helping me into the aisle," she added. "It would have been quite a circus feat for him to help me *and* take the watch from me at once."

"And disappear before the lights came on," Edwin added. "So someone on your left would have had to cause you to trip." He sat back.

Sadie nodded. "And the lights went out at the same moment that I tripped. When they came back on, both the watch and my seatmate were gone. It seems likely that it was more than one person. At least two people had to be working together."

She paused for a moment, thinking, and then burst into laughter.

"Listen to me! A heist! My imagination is running wild."

Edwin's eyes twinkled. "Well, it *is* possible, just maybe not likely."

Sadie shook her head. "Let's just search this train car. Maybe the watch is still here."

They continued their search, working their way backward through the car, checking every nook and cranny they could find.

Beneath the seat in front of 13C, where Sadie had sat, she found a pair of glasses. She picked them up and sat back on her heels in the aisle. The frames were cheap brown plastic, and the lenses were thick. She remembered her seatmate wearing a pair exactly like this.

"Edwin!" she called, and he leaned over her shoulder.

"These are my mystery man's glasses."

"Well, we know he existed, then," Edwin teased.

She lifted the glasses to her face and peered at Edwin through them. She blinked as the realization came to her. He looked as clear and sharp as if the glasses weren't there at all.

"Edwin, these are costume glasses."

6

Sadie's cell phone buzzed as she and Edwin drove back toward town. They'd searched the train car as thoroughly as they could, but—as she'd expected—they found no sign of the watch.

She'd stashed the fake glasses in her purse, and her mind kept coming back to them. Were they part of a disguise? They certainly weren't period appropriate, so they weren't part of the mystery man's costume. It seemed fairly certain that he'd been wearing them to hide his face.

But why? The only reason she could think of was the missing diamond pocket watch. If someone planned to steal something that valuable off a train, they probably wouldn't want other passengers to be able to identify them.

Maybe her heist idea wasn't so crazy after all.

And what about the empty space on the seating chart? Had the mystery man sneaked onto the train, or had Jack just forgotten to write down his name after he'd purchased his ticket?

She glanced down at her phone and saw that she'd received a text from her granddaughter, Sara. She grinned. It had taken her some time to adjust to texting and using a cell phone for every little thing, but it was so nice to be able to "talk" to her grandchildren any time of the day.

Theo and I heard about the treasure hunt. We're in!

Sadie laughed. "It sounds like we have a treasure hunt team forming." She read Sara's message to Edwin.

He chuckled. "That sounds serious."

"Sara's got the social media savviness to track down answers on the go, and Theo's got that natural police detective instinct. I bet they'll have a blast." She opened a reply window.

"I hope so." Edwin gave her a warm smile.

They passed a tall, gaunt figure hobbling along the sidewalk, wearing an outlandish pinstriped suit. Sadie sat up in her seat and peered closer. It couldn't be.

"Edwin, slow down." She pointed out the window. "Isn't that Natty Flats?"

"I'm afraid you'll have to tell me, Sadie," he teased. "I haven't seen him since high school."

Sadie watched without making it obvious as they passed the odd, grizzled figure. Natty was the town eccentric, but more than that, he was the town hermit. Natty never came down from his shack in the mountains without a really good reason.

"I wonder what he's up to." She took in his suit, fedora, and cane.

"Whatever the occasion, he's certainly dressed for it."

Natty didn't raise his head as their car passed. Judging by the intent expression on his face and his purposeful stride, he was a man on a mission.

"Yes—a natty dresser. I always figured that was why he got the nickname," Sadie remarked, settling back in her seat. "He was always a smartly dressed man, but over time, his clothes grew worn out, and the meaning of his name changed."

Edwin nodded. "Maybe he's in town for the festival. Perhaps it brings back fond memories."

"Maybe."

Still, it was odd. Silver Peak hosted events all the time, celebrations that honored their town's past. As far as Sadie could remember, Natty had never showed up for any of them.

Edwin parked in front of the shop. A window on the third floor of the building opened, and Laura Finch, Sadie's cousin, leaned out. "Need help?"

"Hey, Laura!" Sadie smiled. Ever since Laura had moved to Silver Peak—had, in fact, moved into the apartment above Sadie's shop—they had developed a great friendship. Sadie was so glad to have her in Silver Peak and happy her newfound cousin had put down roots in her ancestral hometown. "I think we've got it, but thanks!"

Edwin walked around to the back hatch and opened it. "Should we just put everything in the storeroom?"

"I think that would be best," Sadie agreed. She and Julie could unpack them later, when traffic in the store was slow.

As Edwin reached for a box, his phone buzzed. "I suppose I'd better answer that. Excuse me."

He gave her a quick peck on the cheek, then walked a few paces away. Even at small shows of affection from Edwin, Sadie's heart beat faster. Those tiny gestures were enough to make her day.

Laura came downstairs. "I know you said you didn't need help, but I thought I'd say hi anyway." She glanced over at Edwin, who was engrossed in his conversation. "Are you sure you don't need help?"

Sadie chuckled. "It's only a few boxes, but if you want to be my hired help's replacement, you can."

"Of course!"

The two women each carried a tub into the shop, stowing them neatly in the back room. When they came back outside, Edwin intervened, taking the last box right out of Laura's hands. "You should have waited for me, ladies. I didn't mean for you to do this all by yourselves."

For a moment Sadie thought Laura might revert to her old, helpless manner and let Edwin take over, but then she stepped forward and snatched the box away from him.

"We Wright women can handle a few measly boxes, I think!" Laura joked.

Edwin shook his head and chuckled as Laura carried the box into the shop, and then he turned to Sadie. "I know we were going to have dinner tonight, but I just got a call about the event at the park on Monday. One of our judges has come down with the flu. I need to get back to the office and check our files to see if we have any alternate volunteers."

That was the kind of menial task that any of Edwin's staff could handle, but she knew why he took it on himself. If he called one of his volunteer staff at home, he might interrupt their dinner plans with family. Since Edwin's daughter and her family did not live in Silver Peak, he gladly took on these basic chores to give his staff more time with their families.

Of course, in this case, that meant that Sadie would have her dinner plans interrupted.

She pushed her disappointment aside. Edwin loved Silver Peak as much as she did, and he was doing his best to make this event a success. She shouldn't allow petty feelings into her heart.

"Of course, Edwin. Don't worry about it. I'll see you tomorrow at church."

He touched her shoulder briefly and then climbed into his car. With a wave to both women, he left.

"I'd better get back to work too," Laura said, already heading for the stairs. "See you later!"

Sadie called farewell to Laura and then walked into her shop. Julie walked toward her, ready to lock the front door now that all the boxes were inside.

"What a day!" Julie exclaimed.

"Was it?" Sadie liked the sound of that. It never hurt to have a great sales day.

"Mrs. Slattery came in and bought the Stickley rocker you just finished restoring, and we had streams of tourists in and out. I suppose if I'd been to the party last night, I might have recognized some of them—but when my husband's on call, our best-laid plans go right out the window." Julie flipped the sign on the door around to read Closed.

"Any other big sales?" Sadie began running the register tape.

"No, mostly small purchases. Something strange did happen, though. Some guy came in and wanted to root around in that box of photos you have behind the counter, you know, the ones leftover from when you made the Collin Malloy display? But I told him he'd have to come back. I knew you hadn't priced them yet." Julie slipped off her flats and rolled her feet against the bare wood floorboards.

"Go on home, Julie," Sadie said sympathetically. "I'll close everything up. I didn't mean to be gone for so long, but I got sidetracked at the train station." She gave her employee a wry look and added, "No pun intended. Honest!"

Julie looked at her a moment and then burst into laughter. "Sadie, I never know if I should laugh or groan at some of your jokes!"

Sadie smiled. "But seriously, now. You have two boys at home who are probably tired and wanting their dinner."

"Tired and dirty and wanting dinner, and probably fighting each other too," Julie admitted with a laugh. "Are you sure you don't mind?"

"Not at all. Go on home." Sadie pulled the register tape off and began counting the cash.

Julie gave her one last wave and walked out the door. Sadie finished totaling the day's receipts. It was a pretty decent Saturday for sales, helped a great deal by Mrs. Slattery's big-ticket purchase and Grace Elliott's brooch, even counting the loss of the poinsettia pin. Sadie put the money in the vinyl bag she used for deposits and began closing up the rest of the store.

Lights on in the front display area. Check. The connecting door between the Antique Mine and Arbuckle's locked. Check. Jewelry case locked. Check.

As Sadie stepped back from the case, her foot brushed up against something hard. She stooped down and peered at the wooden floor. There it was—the missing poinsettia brooch. It must have fallen while Julie was helping Mrs. Elliott.

Sadie scooped up the brooch, and a sparkle caught her eye. She bent down further, going onto all fours to search beneath the cabinet. A diamond earring had fallen down there too.

She grabbed it and set it alongside the brooch, in the palm of her hand. Then she sat back on her heels and gazed at them both.

The diamond earring was unfamiliar, not part of her stock. It was a marquis-cut, contemporary design—like nothing she'd buy or sell. A customer must have lost it. Her costume buyers liked fanciful designs, the more whimsical the better, and this diamond was strictly modern—clean-cut and cold.

She paused. Shouldn't a diamond have more warmth to it? Comparing this earring to the pocket watch she'd held briefly last night, it seemed like this jewel lacked that special fire that real diamonds had. She breathed on it, and the jewel fogged briefly. Definitely not real diamonds.

She turned the earring over. A hallmark was stamped into the silver setting. "HK." That did not ring a bell at all.

She stood, her joints protesting a little more than they should, and tucked the poinsettia brooch back into the case, locking it securely.

What to do with the earring? Was it valuable? Should she take it to the police department?

No, if a customer had lost it, then they would probably come to the Antique Mine first to look for it. She opened the register and placed the earring beneath the cash drawer. That would keep it secure until she could find out more about it or track down the owner.

Sadie walked through the shop, turning out the lights as she went, and out the front door, locking it behind her. The evening air was crisp and cold, and a keen wind ruffled her hair. She breathed deeply, relishing the scent of fires burning in all the fireplaces in her town. Everyone was tucking themselves inside for the night.

Sadie decided she didn't feel like cooking that evening, so she turned toward Arbuckle's, planning to pick up a sandwich.

Across the street, a ladder was propped up against the side of the building, providing access to the roof. Spike's shop exterior and roof had been damaged in a storm a few weeks earlier, and judging by the ladder, he had been in the process of examining it himself. Sadie tilted her head to one side as she looked. The ladder was old and rickety, and as Sadie walked down the street, she could see it rocking gently in the wind.

She had a much nicer self-stabilizing ladder in her garage that T.R. had bought a few years ago. Maybe she should ask Spike if he'd like to borrow it. It would probably be much safer than the one he was using, and she'd hate for him to fall and get injured.

She crossed the street to Spike's shop. The door was closed and locked, and the lights were off downstairs. He must be in his apartment. She took the outside stairs and knocked on the door.

Spike opened the door. He was a tall, lean man with a vaguely haunted air about him. He was dressed, as usual, in blue jeans and a leather bomber jacket, even though he was indoors. "Hey, Sadie," he said, smiling shyly.

Sadie smiled warmly in return. He wasn't the most talkative person she knew, and sometimes she felt like she needed to encourage him to keep going, as she used to do with reluctant students in her class. "Hi, Spike," she began. "Just wanted to say how much I'm looking forward to the Skylarks' concert later this week." She mentioned Spike's successful country band by name.

"Thanks." Spike gave a half smile, but he didn't say more than that. He blinked, as if waiting for her to speak again.

"Hey, man!" Another man's voice echoed from inside the apartment. "If we're gonna make it, we need to go."

"On my way," Spike called over his shoulder. He turned back to Sadie. "We're just heading out to rehearse right now, Sadie. Thanks for stopping by."

Spike's friend came to the doorway, his face cast in half-shadow. Sadie blinked, feeling like she was seeing a ghost.

He pushed past Spike, extending his hand. "Hi. I'm Robert Smith. Have we met before?"

Sadie could only stare at him. With that sandy hair and those ice-blue eyes, he was a dead ringer for Collin Malloy.

7

Sadie stood before both men, unable to speak. She must have looked completely foolish, standing there with her mouth open, but for a moment she couldn't frame her thoughts.

Collin Malloy had died in the 1930s, but this young man's resemblance was uncanny, right down to the cleft in his chin.

"No, I don't believe we have," she finally managed, shaking his hand.

"Sadie owns the antique store across the street, Robbie," Spike said. "You should go check it out."

"It's a pleasure to meet you," Robert said. He turned to Spike. "Are we going to be late for rehearsal?"

Spike glanced down at his watch. "Probably. We gotta go." Spike gave Sadie a nod. "Sorry to run, but we've got a big rehearsal for the gig on Friday night."

"Of course." Sadie took a step backward, preparing to leave. "Are you playing with the Skylarks, Robert?"

"Call me Robbie. Everyone does." He gave her another self-assured half grin, and Sadie was momentarily lost in his blue eyes. He seemed so familiar, but then of course he would, if he reminded her of Collin Malloy. "Yeah, while I'm blowing through town, I'm hanging out with Spike and gigging with the Skylarks."

"One of the best bass players on the West Coast," Spike put in. "We're glad he could come out and play." He looked at his watch again. "Thanks for stopping by, Sadie. We'll see you on Friday."

"See you then."

She made her way down the side staircase, her footsteps ringing out as they struck each wrought-iron step. A dozen questions swirled through her mind. Sadie tucked her hands in her jacket pockets and trotted across the street again to Arbuckle's.

Fifteen minutes later, her dinner in a plastic sack in one hand, Sadie climbed into the Tahoe and started the engine. As the vehicle warmed up, she leaned her head back against the seat rest. She'd been so surprised at seeing a man who looked like Collin Malloy that she'd forgotten to ask Spike if he wanted to borrow her ladder. What had she been thinking?

As Sadie drove home, the sun sank lower and lower over the mountain peaks, gilding the summits and valleys with a warm, golden glow. She cracked her driver's-side window and breathed the fresh, cool night air.

"Well, there's nothing to do except ask him later," Sadie muttered.

She switched on the radio, and Patsy Cline's sweet, husky voice filled the air, singing "Crazy." Sadie laughed. The song certainly suited how she felt lately, losing a diamond pocket watch just moments after finding it. Sadie hummed along with the song as she drew closer to home. Hank would want his evening walk before it got too dark. And she was hungry. Her grilled panini sandwich was making the interior of the Tahoe smell divine.

So much had happened in the space of one day, and she still wasn't sure what to make of any of it. Where had that watch gone? And who on earth was that mystery man on the train?

———

It was Sunday, and there was nothing better on a Sunday morning than to worship at Campfire Chapel.

Sadie settled into the pew beside Edwin, who looked distinguished as usual in a dark wool suit and conservative tie. She smoothed her casual denim skirt and waved to Roz, who had just entered.

"Hey, Sadie! Hey, Edwin!" Roz sang out as she squeezed into the pew. "Roscoe doesn't feel well today. Mild stomachache. I told him he ate too many of those bacon-wrapped shrimp the other night."

Sadie laughed and swatted Roz's arm with her bulletin. "Be nice to Roscoe. Those bacon-wrapped shrimp were delicious!"

Jeanne Sweeting entered the sanctuary, looking elegant. When she spotted Sadie, she waved. Sadie excused herself and walked over to greet the pastor's wife.

Jeanne smiled broadly, enfolding Sadie in a warm hug. "Have you started your treasure hunt yet?"

Sadie laughed. "I think I have a team assembled. Theo and Sara texted me yesterday to say they want to hunt too."

"Well, you'll be a formidable team." Jeanne patted her shoulder and started to walk off, then turned back. "Oh! I almost forgot to tell you, but I did find out who that man was speaking to the other night. Don got an e-mail from a woman named Darcy

Burke, who wants him to officiate at her wedding. I saw her picture in the e-mail, and I'm fairly certain it's her. Of course, it was dark—but I think she's the girl I saw."

Well, that confirmed Sadie's suspicion that Darcy had met her mystery man that night. What were they talking about? Were they exchanging information—or the watch?

"When is Darcy's wedding? Did Don agree to officiate?"

"Yes. It's on Wednesday. It's very short notice, but she said her previous officiate was having emergency surgery and wouldn't be available." Jeanne frowned slightly. "I hope the poor man is okay."

"I'll say a quick prayer for him today."

Jeanne flashed her bright smile. "Me too."

The musicians at the front of the chapel began tuning their instruments, and Jeanne made her way to the front pew.

Spike was on stage, tuning his violin. Sadie thrilled to the sound as he drew his bow across the strings. He was an excellent fiddle player, and the service was always so much richer when he played. She glanced around the pews. Robbie Smith was nowhere to be found. She supposed he wasn't into church music, but she'd wanted to point him out to Edwin and see if he also saw the uncanny resemblance to Malloy.

Near the end of the service, Edwin leaned over. "I still haven't found a replacement judge for tomorrow's games," he whispered. "I know we were supposed to have Sunday lunch together, but I really need to find someone to volunteer. I'm sorry. I know it's rude—"

"No problem, Edwin." She patted his arm. This was a matter of conscience for him, and they would have the chance to have Sunday lunch again next week.

Edwin gave her a grateful smile, and as the music ended, they filed out of the chapel. Spike walked on ahead of the group pouring out of the lovely restored clapboard building, his fiddle case bumping against his leg with each stride. Sadie shaded her eyes and watched him head back toward town.

With a wave to Edwin and to Roz, Sadie headed toward her Tahoe. It was such a lovely day, cool and bright, and Hank would love a hike in the mountains after lunch.

Just as she reached her car, Jane Remington, owner of the Silver Peak Bed-and-Breakfast, called her name and hurried toward her. Sadie turned toward her, keys in her hand.

"Sadie! Do you have any raisins? Please tell me you do." Jane's face was drawn into tight lines.

Sadie laughed in surprise. "Raisins? I think so. Why on earth do you need raisins?"

"Well, you know how I advertise my oatmeal raisin scones as part of our continental breakfast?"

"Rightly so. You're famous for them."

"I woke up this morning and had less than a quarter of a cup of raisins in the cupboard. I tried to substitute blueberries in the scones, because I have a whole bag of them frozen from this summer, but my guests wouldn't hear of it. They were really upset, since that was what we advertised." She threw her graceful hands up in the air. "The Market is closed and you know how I hate having to drive down to one of the big box stores. And would you believe none of my neighbors have any raisins on hand?"

"I am pretty sure I have a few extra boxes. I stocked up the last time they were on sale. You know I like to shop in bulk." She smiled and patted Jane's shoulder. "Do you want to follow me out to the house to fetch them?"

Jane relaxed in relief. "That'd be great. I promised I'd have the scones at tea this afternoon."

"Follow me. We'll save your scones."

Jane hurried to her car, and Sadie climbed into her Tahoe and headed for home.

Jane parked behind her in the driveway, and Sadie ushered her into the house, letting Hank out at the same time.

"You wait right here. I'll come back with the raisins." Sadie scurried to the kitchen and dug two large boxes out of the pantry, then brought them back to Jane.

Jane began rummaging in her pocket. "How much do I owe you for these?"

"Don't be ridiculous! What are a few raisins among friends?" Sadie joked.

"Thanks, friend. I'll bring some unwanted blueberry scones to you at the shop tomorrow." Jane yawned and stretched. "Well, back to the salt mines. Honestly, I hate to say it, but I don't think I've ever had guests this demanding. The husband is constantly talking on his phone. Loudly. I don't spy on my guests, and make it a habit to respect their privacy, but I can't help but hear everything he says!"

"If they're the couple I'm thinking of, they were pretty demanding when they came into the shop the other day too," Sadie commiserated. The Elliotts didn't seem to be making any friends in Silver Peak.

"I'm a little worried, actually." Jane lowered her voice even though they were the only people in the house and grabbed Sadie's arm. "Please don't say anything to anyone, but I'm afraid they won't be able to pay their bill. The way his phone conversations keep going…"

The Elliotts were, at the very least, overdrawn. Hadn't she had trouble running their credit card? The wheels began turning in Sadie's mind, but she didn't want to burden Jane, who seemed harassed enough as it was. "If they can't pay, is it worth catering to their every whim?"

"Our business thrives on word of mouth." Jane shrugged. "One bad review posted online could cost us valuable customers. So even though I'm worried he'll skip out on the bill, and even though they aren't always polite, I have to keep being a good hostess."

Jane rolled her eyes, and Sadie laughed. "Well, it will be over soon."

"As soon as they check out, I'm going to celebrate by soaking in a nice hot bubble bath," Jane admitted with a laugh. "Well, I had better run along. See you later, Sadie. I'll bring some scones by for you, I promise."

Sadie showed Jane out the door, ushered Hank back in, and began to make lunch in anticipation of her family coming over in a little while.

It was a bit of a leap, but could the Elliotts somehow be connected to the disappearance of the pocket watch? They were certainly in some kind of financial trouble, and a watch as valuable as Collin Malloy's would solve a lot of money problems. And they'd been near her on the train when the lights went out.

Sadie shook her head. Just because they were demanding and rude, it didn't mean they'd feel entitled to take a diamond pocket watch that wasn't theirs. As the doorbell rang, Sadie decided to push thoughts of the watch aside and spend time with her family.

Later, as Sadie gathered with Alice, Theo, and Sara around the table, she said a prayer of thanksgiving for the bounty of food and companionship they shared. As soon as she finished, Theo grabbed a basket of rolls and helped himself to three at once.

"Theo! Manners," Alice reminded him gently.

"Sorry, Mom," Theo mumbled, his face turning red. "Grandma just makes the best dinner rolls."

"Theo's right." Sara drizzled honey over the buttered roll on her plate.

"I guess I'd better get some before they're gone, then," Alice said, reaching for the basket of rolls.

The lunch passed quickly, with Theo eating three servings of chicken casserole, and Sadie delighted in every moment with her grandkids. They were growing up so quickly.

When the meal was over, the kids took Hank out for a hike, and Alice helped Sadie clean up the kitchen. While they worked, Sadie recounted finding—and losing—the watch on the train.

When she'd finished, Alice stared at her. "So it's real? Wow." She was quiet for a moment. "If you didn't drop it, then it must have been taken from your hand. That's the only way it makes sense."

"I don't know," Sadie admitted, taking a thoughtful sip of water. "I don't remember dropping it, but I don't remember someone taking it from me either. If it was a planned theft, it feels like a pretty elaborate scheme, especially considering I found the watch completely by accident."

"What about the lights?" Alice asked. "Someone could have turned them off on purpose."

"Unless it was a mechanical fault," Sadie put in. "Jack Fitzgerald hasn't totally ruled that out." She placed the clean casserole pan in the dish drainer. "There! That's the last of it."

The back door opened and Theo and Sara appeared in the kitchen doorway, cheeks pink with cold and excitement.

"I thought you were hiking," Alice said, looking at her watch. "You were only gone for fifteen minutes."

"We want to plan our treasure hunt strategy with Grandma," Sara explained.

"Okay, what should we do first?" Sadie asked.

Theo narrowed his eyes. "Well, I think we need to research the watch. We need to know what it looks like. I mean, not that there are lots of diamond pocket watches hanging out in Silver Peak. But still, we have to start with the facts."

Sadie grinned. Theo was talking, and acting, like the detective he wanted to become. "I agree."

"So does this mean a trip to the library?" Sara sounded elaborately casual, but Sadie knew better. Sara was smitten with Anthony Parker, who was the assistant to the head librarian, Kimama Temoke. His charming British accent was certainly romantic-sounding, Sadie had to admit.

"First stop, the library." Sadie pronounced. "The treasure hunt will officially start the moment we walk in the doors."

8

THE NEXT MORNING MARKED THE OPENING FESTIVITIES TO celebrate the new train. Sadie looked forward to Tuesday afternoon, when Sara and Theo would join her to research Collin Malloy's watch at the public library, but in the meantime, she had work to do.

Sadie methodically counted out the cash in the register, enjoying the expectant hush of the store before she opened the doors for business. She hoped this past weekend's high traffic meant that she could expect a busy week.

She lifted the cash drawer in the register to slide the deposit bag underneath, and as she did, the earring she'd found on Saturday caught the light. She took the earring out and examined it again in the bright morning sunlight. It definitely didn't have the kind of fire she had come to expect from diamonds, but it was exceptionally pretty and well-made. Sadie squinted, hoping that a closer look would give her some kind of answer about its origin, but she was at the limit of her expertise.

She'd hang on to it until someone claimed it, but what if it really was valuable? If so, then she should take it to the police station. On the other hand, if it was merely a nicely done costume piece, there was probably no need to bother the police with it.

The door opened, and Julie strolled in, wearing a vivid red cape with a bunch of appliquéd cherries at the neckline. "Morning, Sadie!"

"Morning, Julie! How was your Sunday?"

"Great! I actually got to sleep in a little, and then we all gorged ourselves on cinnamon rolls." Julie nodded toward Sadie's hand. "What have you got there?"

Sadie held out the earring in her palm. "I found this on the floor when I was closing up on Saturday. Do you recognize it?"

Julie peered at the earring, touching it lightly with the tip of her finger. "No, I don't. It's very nice, though. Do you think one of our customers dropped it?"

"I think so. I actually found it beside the poinsettia brooch, which had rolled under the jewelry case."

Julie whooped. "Oh, thank heaven for that. I was so worried about that pin."

Sadie grinned. "See? I told you it would all work out just fine. I think, though, that I am going to walk this little piece over to Bless Our Souls to see if Fred or Debbie Sunshine might be able to give me some information on it."

"Oh, I just noticed that they're closed today," Julie said. "I think they might be on a buying trip."

"Good to know," Sadie said. She thought for a moment. "I'll go see Joe Martinez instead. I know it's not a real diamond, but maybe Joe can tell me if it's valuable or not. If it is, then I am going to take it to the police station."

"Good plan." Julie removed her cape, revealing a charming 1940s shirtwaist dress underneath. "I'm ready to start, so feel free to go now, if you'd like."

"Trying to get rid of me?" Sadie quipped.

Julie laughed. "You know me better than that."

"All right, then." Sadie smiled and grabbed her coffee. She didn't even need to worry about putting on her jacket, since she hadn't taken it off since her arrival that morning. "See you in a bit."

As she went out the front door, she flipped the shop's sign to Open. Then she drove past the downtown area, east toward the fringes of town where Main Street became Route 65, to the Plaza, a small strip mall that had been built some years before. The area lacked the graceful charm of Silver Peak's historic downtown, but it was home to shops such as Joe's, including a pack-and-ship service, a nail salon, and the town's only dry cleaner.

Joe's Pawn Shop occupied the end of the Plaza, the plate-glass window lit by a red neon Open sign. The cinder-block building, like the rest of the mall, was long and low but neat and looked like it had had a fresh coat of paint in the last month. As Sadie approached, she spied Joe Martinez placing bicycles out on the front rack. She parked her Tahoe and climbed out.

"Hi, Sadie!" Joe called, his dark eyes twinkling. "I don't see you here too often. What can I help you with?"

Sadie fished in her pocket and drew out the earring. "What do you make of this? I found it in my shop, but it's definitely not part of my stock."

"*Hmm.*" Joe picked up the earring and held it close, closing one eye to get a better look. "I can't tell. It sure doesn't have the warmth of a diamond. Want me to take a look at it with my loupe?"

"Do you mind? I'm pretty sure too that it's not real, but if it's valuable, I want to turn it over to the sheriff."

"Not at all." He ushered her into the shop. "Come on inside. I'd offer you some coffee, but I see you brought your own."

"Well, I'll probably need a refill by the time I leave," Sadie admitted with a chuckle.

Joe moved down the front aisle, and Sadie was impressed with how neat and organized his store was. A glittering guitar held a place of honor, displayed with an amp that looked brand-new. Sadie didn't know much about instruments—at least not modern ones—but this guitar looked like something a rock star would use.

Joe noticed her stopping to admire the instrument. "You in the market for a guitar?" he asked, half-teasing. "That's a 1953 Les Paul Goldtop. Pretty rare. I'll cut you a deal on it, if you want it."

He winked, and Sadie laughed. "I don't know the first thing about guitars."

With one last admiring look at the guitar, she met him at the counter in the back of the shop.

"All right, let's see what we're looking at." Holding the earring up for a better, closer look, he picked up his loupe and peered at it intently. "It's a cubic zirconia," he pronounced. "Definitely not a diamond, like you said. I must say, it's pretty good for a zirconia. Most of the ones that I see in the shop are obvious fakes. This one lacked the kind of depth you see in a diamond at first glance, but I bet you could fool a lot of people with it."

Sadie set her coffee cup down on the counter. "Do you think it's worth anything? I mean, should I take it over to the police department for safekeeping?"

"I don't know that you need to bother the police about it." Joe placed the loupe aside and flipped over the earring, then glanced up at Sadie with a thoughtful expression. "The hallmark says HK.

This might be a Hannah-Kristoff piece. They make really good costume jewelry—almost as expensive as the real deal."

"Why would someone pay almost as much for a fake diamond as a real one?"

Joe shrugged and handed the earring back to Sadie. She tucked it carefully in the pocket of her fleece jacket. "I hear a lot of shifty stories in my line of work. The most common reason to have a good fake piece of jewelry is for insurance fraud. Say, for example, you have a really nice diamond pendant, and you insure it for thousands of dollars. Then you have a fake made to look just like it. You sell the real one under the table, but keep the fake around for a while, just to convince people that it's yours and it's authentic. Then you claim it's been stolen and file an insurance claim." Joe shook his head, reaching past his crowded desk for the twelve-cup coffeemaker and its glass carafe. "Refill?"

"Please." Sadie unscrewed the lid of her travel mug and breathed in deeply, relishing the aroma of the fresh brew. "That happens in the antique world too. So this piece could have been made to perpetrate a fraud."

Joe helped himself to a cup and leaned against the desk. "Oh, I'm sure that's not the case. It's probably just a really nice fake for someone who couldn't quite afford the real thing. Or remember when they remade all of Jacqueline Onassis's jewelry and sold it through infomercials? It could be something like that."

The bell above the shop door jingled, and Natty Flats entered, resplendent in a burgundy velvet suit and frilly cravat. Sadie tried not to stare, but it was really difficult to remember her manners.

While lifting her coffee mug to take a sip, she glanced at Natty from under her half-closed lids. She blinked and looked again.

No, she hadn't dreamed that suit up. Natty bent down to look at something on the bottom shelf, the tails of his suit jacket sweeping the dusty floor.

"Hey there, Mr. Flats," Joe called. "You lookin' for something particular?"

"Not buying today, Joe. Selling." Natty straightened slowly. When he looked toward the counter, he spied Sadie standing there and froze. "When you ain't busy anymore."

"Oh, don't mind me, Mr. Flats." Sadie gave him a friendly smile. "I was just having a little coffee with Joe."

"I'll wait." Natty stood, his shoulders slightly stooped, and set his jaw. His bright blue eyes darted back and forth under his bushy white eyebrows, watching Sadie as well as the door.

Sadie stood. "Oh, I'd hate to make you wait. Joe and I were done. I'll get out of your hair."

She turned back to Joe. "Thank you for the coffee and the information. Are you coming to any of the events later on in the week?"

"I'm not sure just yet." Joe smiled. "But maybe. Have a good day, Sadie."

Sadie wound her way back through the aisle, sliding past Natty to the front door. "Are you coming to any of the 1930s events this week, Mr. Flats?"

"Events?" Natty spat the word out like a wad of chewing tobacco. "What events?"

His right hand, gnarled with age, was tucked protectively around a small brown bag he held tightly against his chest. If he wasn't coming into town because the railway had opened or for the festival, what was he here for? Was it to sell whatever was in that brown bag to Joe? She felt sure Joe would give him a good price for it, whatever it was.

"The events celebrating the reopening of the Mountain Crest Railway," Sadie explained with an encouraging smile. "Only now it's called the Silver Peak Scenic Railway."

"I remember that railroad." Natty nodded, his eyes taking on a dreamy, distant look. "Remember it well from the old days. You say they've reopened it?"

"Yes, sir." Even though she was a grown woman and a grandma, and even though folks in Silver Peak were very casual, Natty was her elder, and she couldn't help calling him Mr. Flats or sir. "They're having events here in town all week."

Natty's blue eyes narrowed, and he rubbed his hand over his clean-shaven chin. "Well, now, that does sound interesting. I miss that old Engine No. 2. Had some good times in the rail yard when I was just a little sprout. I was the fastest delivery boy in town, you know." He straightened, as though proud. "Not all the kids got to handle the things I did. They gave them to me because they trusted me."

Natty's wistful expression closed like a shutter as he refocused on her again. "You were leavin'? I got some business to take care of." His tone signaled that he was no longer in the mood for nostalgia.

"Of course. I don't want to take up your time." She smiled and nodded. "Hope to see you later this week, Mr. Flats."

His only reply was a curt grunt as he turned toward Joe and the counter at the back of the shop. With one last look at his hunched figure, Sadie left.

Out on the sidewalk, she paused a moment, taking a long sip from her coffee. Natty rarely ambled into town, but his brusque behavior was not unusual. She had spoken to him only a few times over the years, but he always struck her as someone who had other things to do than socialize. She got the feeling he didn't suffer polite conversation gladly.

She drove back toward the Antique Mine, relishing the view of the sunlight peeking over the mountains. At least now she knew that the earring was a very well-done fake. Interesting what Joe had said about insurance fraud and fake jewels. She had heard of such things, especially in regard to passing off fake antiques as the real deal, but it just showed that as a pawnshop owner, Joe had definitely seen a more colorful side of life. This was why it was so refreshing to work with so many different people.

She had gleaned all kinds of interesting information from booksellers, thrift shop owners, other antiques experts, and folks running stalls down at the flea market. She wouldn't give up this career, not, as her mother used to say, for all the tea in China.

As she rounded the corner near the Antique Mine, the sight of Spike's building reminded her that she had yet to offer him the use of her ladder to fix his roof. Well, there was no time like the present.

Sadie parked her car and walked over to Spike's shop.

Maybe Robert Smith, Collin Malloy's look-alike, would be there.

9

As Sadie opened the door to the music shop, the rich sound of acoustic country music tumbled out into the street. She poked her head inside, smiling.

Spike and Robert Smith had set up a stage in the middle of the store, Spike playing guitar and Robert plucking away at an upright bass. Spike's clear baritone rang out as he sang the words to "In the Sweet By and By," with Robbie's high, lonesome tenor adding harmony. As he came to the end of the verse, they stopped playing. It was always so amazing that musicians, even when just jamming, knew when to stop and start together. It seemed like such a basic thing, really, but it never ceased to astonish her.

She stepped inside and closed the door behind her.

"I thought that was good." Robert plucked a string of his bass.

"Maybe bring it down a step or two. Felt like I was straining a bit on some of those high notes," Spike replied, frowning as he retuned his guitar. "How about G?"

"Sure. Ready to go again?" Robert rested the bass against his shoulder.

"Yep." Spike picked the opening notes then glanced up, catching sight of Sadie. "Oh, hi, Sadie. Are we making too much noise? Can you hear us over at your place?"

"I certainly hope so," Sadie said with a laugh. "You two sound great. That song was one of my mother's favorites."

"We're just playing around." Spike set his guitar on the stand beside him. "Practicing for our gigs later in the week. The rest of the Skylarks have day jobs, so we're jamming."

"I thought we sounded pretty good," Robert protested, looking at Sadie. She was again struck by a sense of familiarity, due to his resemblance to Collin Malloy. "Even playing these old beat-up things. Now, if we had some of the gear we used to pack in the old days... or some of those axes you see at auction."

"Axes?" Sadie asked.

Spike chuckled. "A lot of guitar and bass players call their instruments that. Not sure why."

"Ah! Well, I am sure anything Spike sells here is excellent," Sadie gave Spike a warm smile. "Though now that you mention it, I saw a beautiful guitar at Joe's Pawn Shop today. A Les Paul Goldtop, he called it."

"Really?" Spike's eyes glittered with sudden keen interest. "Did he say what year?"

"It was from the 1950s. I can't recall the actual year. Why—is that good?"

"It could be awesome," Robert piped up. "Those Les Paul Goldtops from the early fifties are impressive instruments. Expensive too."

"Then you should go check it out. I bet Joe would let you play it, just for kicks."

Spike smiled at her. "Thanks, Sadie. You're sure we're not being too loud?"

"Oh no, not at all. I just stopped by to ask you something. I noticed you had an old ladder out yesterday, I assume to check the damage the storm did to your roof. I just wondered if you'd like to borrow my ladder—it's much newer and more stable, and it'd be no trouble to bring it into town for you."

A sheepish expression crossed Spike's face. "Yeah, that ladder is probably an accident waiting to happen. But the roof damage is beyond my skill, so I decided to call Ardis Fleagle and have him come fix it." He smiled again. "So don't worry. I won't be back on that ladder any time soon."

Sadie laughed. "I'm glad to hear it."

Robert shook his head, looking amused. "Spike Harris? Pay someone else to fix something? Wow, you folks here in Silver Peak must really take pride in your old buildings and stuff. I guess it is a lot different than in LA."

Sadie nodded. "You're right about that. We take pride in our old buildings and our history. But don't worry, Robbie. We don't take ourselves that seriously." She winked.

Robert threw his head back and laughed. "Well, in any case, Spike seems to fit right in here."

"You could say we've adopted him," she teased. "Well, I'll let you get back to your music. Let me know if you change your mind about the ladder, Spike."

"Sure thing, Sadie." Spike was already tuning his guitar. Robert began plucking a rhythmic figure on the bass strings.

Sadie waved and showed herself out, with the music fading as she closed the door behind her. Outside, on the sidewalk, she took several deep breaths of the clear mountain air. Even though it was late into the morning, Main Street remained quiet and relatively empty. She could smell the heady, pungent aroma of coffee roasting from Arbuckle's and briefly debated stopping in to pick up another coffee and a mid-morning snack. But no, she'd better hold out at least until after lunch.

She stuffed her free hand into her coat pocket, the other hand clutching her empty travel mug. The cubic zirconia rasped against her fingertips. She should go back to the Antique Mine and put the earring safely back into the cash register.

If Sadie could lose something as big, and as valuable, as a diamond pocket watch, she certainly didn't trust herself with an earring.

"If you don't need me, Sadie, I'll be going." Julie tugged on her coat. "Sorry it was such a slow day. Maybe tomorrow will be better."

"Mondays are never a big sales day, at least this time of year," Sadie replied with a shrug. Ups and downs were just the nature of retail. "I hope sales pick up later in the week when some of the bigger events take place. Have a good night!"

Julie smiled and stretched on her gloves. "You too. See you in the morning." She wound her way down the aisle. Her high-heeled boots clicked across the wooden floor as she exited through the front door.

Sadie counted out the last of the cash, dividing it into two neat piles, one to be deposited and one to be used as the start of tomorrow's register. She tucked the deposit envelope into her purse and started the rest of her closing routine.

Sadie mulled over the day's events as she turned off lights and straightened merchandise. Tomorrow would be fun, researching Collin Malloy's watch with Theo and Sara. Edwin had the right idea when he planned the treasure hunt as part of the week's festivities—it was a nostalgic and exciting way to make Silver Peak's history come alive. If only the watch hadn't been taken right out of her hand...

She glanced down at her own wristwatch. It was well past six o'clock now, and she really should hurry. Hank would be waiting for her, and she was growing hungrier by the second.

She had checked that the back door was locked and turned to go back up front when a shadow flickered across the far wall. Sadie paused.

What was that?

She had turned off all the lights except for the few strategically placed ones they used to illuminate displays at night. Maybe something outside had moved and cast a strange silhouette on the wall. She took another step forward and paused.

The shadow moved again, and a definite sound of footsteps, slow and deliberate, rang out. Sadie's breath caught in her throat.

Someone else was in the store with her.

10

Sadie's mouth went dry. Could she really be confronting a thief right here in Silver Peak?

The shadow dropped down the wall, and Sadie spied a hunched figure crawling around on the floor. Yes, no doubt about it, someone else was with her in the store.

She bent down and grasped a parasol from the umbrella stand in the doorway. It was a Victorian piece, with a lovely rosewood handle, from an estate she'd handled outside of Colorado Springs. Sadie inched forward, the parasol clutched tightly in her grasp. She gave it a mental apology for wielding such a beautiful piece of functional art as a weapon.

The hunched figure on the floor was smaller than Sadie, and kept muttering. Some of Sadie's panic subsided as she took in the strangeness of the situation. Wouldn't a thief be as quiet as possible? Wouldn't a thief be stealthy too? Sadie continued her slow progress toward the register, remaining cautious even though her fear was fading.

As she drew close enough that she could strike out if she needed to, the hunched figure sat back.

"It's not here." The stranger rose, stepping further into the light. "Oh, it's you." The woman pushed back the hood of her coat. It was Grace Elliott, wearing a fur-lined parka and a harassed expression. "Look, I need your help finding something."

Sadie nearly dropped the parasol as relief coursed through her body, but she managed to place it gently to one side. She fought the urge to laugh. "Help you find what?"

"I lost an earring here. Or at least I think I did." Grace Elliott sank to her hands and knees again, patting around on the bare wooden floor with her gloved hands. "It must have slipped out of my pocket when I was looking at your jewelry. Have you seen it? Why is it so *dark* in here?"

For a moment, Sadie just stared as Grace rummaged around on her hands and knees. Any other customer would have come back during daylight hours, or called on the phone, or done anything but what Grace Elliot was doing right now.

Sadie couldn't contain her desire to laugh any longer. It was all so silly. She threw back her head and laughed. "You do realize that we're closed?" she finally managed, wiping tears of mirth from her eyes.

Grace finally rose to her feet, frowning. "You're closed? But it's only 5:00."

"Well, we closed at five. It's actually after six now. How did you get in?" Sadie asked. Julie had locked the door behind her when she left.

"Through the door to that coffee shop," Grace said. "The door was open, so I assumed you were too."

Sadie shook her head. She hadn't gotten around to locking the door to Arbuckle's yet. Grace must have come into the shop while Sadie was checking the back door.

"I had to come back and search while Thomas was busy with his phone conference," Grace continued. "If he finds out I lost another piece of jewelry, he'll kill me."

"Well, I might have found your earring," Sadie said. "Can you describe it?" She flipped a light switch and moved toward the cash register.

"It's a diamond earring, very modern setting."

Sadie paused in the act of opening the cash register drawer. "Are you sure it was a diamond one?"

Grace sniffed. "Of course it was diamond. My husband bought it for me."

Sadie chose not to contradict her and unlocked the register. She reached under the drawer and pulled out the cubic zirconia. "Is this it?"

"Yes." Grace grabbed it away from her and tucked it in her pocket.

"It's such a unique piece." Sadie closed the cash drawer and locked the register with its little brass key. "Where did—"

"It *is* a unique piece. And it's mine. Now that I have it back, I'll be going." Grace strode over to the front door, all business now that she had completed her mission. "The door's locked. Let me out."

Sadie retrieved her keys and opened the door. After Grace left, she locked it again and sat on a nearby rocking chair, shaking her head ruefully.

Most people wouldn't brew a pot of coffee at eight o'clock at night, Sadie reflected as she puttered around her kitchen. In fact, most people would be surprised that she could drink caffeine this late in the day and still be able to sleep well at night. Sadie knew it was a rare blessing, and, as much as she enjoyed her coffee, she was thankful for it.

She poured the steaming brew into a Jadeite coffee mug and padded into her living room. Hank raised his head. He was already curled onto his favorite large pillow by the fireplace and gave his tail a brief wag as she walked past him and set her coffee mug on the oak table beside her favorite reading chair.

She couldn't stop thinking about the mystery man from the train. He was the most obvious candidate for stealing the watch, but how had he disappeared so quickly? How had he known the watch was there in the first place?

Most importantly, who was he?

Sadie was completely stymied on where to begin looking for him. She had no name, nowhere to begin researching him and tracking him down.

Her best bet was to find Darcy, who had been seen talking to him after the train returned to the station. Maybe Darcy knew him or would be able to give Sadie more information.

Since it was too late to call Jack Fitzgerald about Darcy, she picked up the Collin Malloy biography she'd brought back downstairs earlier, and settled into her chair. Sadie flipped through the pages again, pausing to look at the pictures once more.

She stared at a picture of Malloy, taken outside the premiere of one of his Hollywood films. He stood behind a bank of large round microphones, his top hat cocked over one eyebrow.

It was so odd how much Robert Smith looked like Collin Malloy. Uncanny. It wasn't just her imagination; it was real. She checked the index for a sign of any children or family of Malloy's, but didn't see anything. She skimmed the last few chapters of the book to make sure, but saw no sign that Collin Malloy had married or even been thinking about marriage. Of course, he didn't have to be married to have a child, but surely that kind of scandal would have made the book, and there was no hint of it.

If only she could rid herself of the notion that Robert Smith was somehow related to Malloy. She closed the book and drummed her fingers on the cover.

When she had questions about an antique, and needed help identifying one, she would seek out an expert. Violet McKay, the author of this book, was Malloy's biographer and an expert on his life. Perhaps with McKay's help, Sadie could piece together his lineage. She turned to the "About the Author" page and found McKay's e-mail address.

Sadie opened a new e-mail on her phone and began to type.
Dear Ms. McKay,

I live in Silver Peak, Colorado, and we're having a few events here this week that celebrate some aspects of Collin Malloy's career. As I learn more about him, I wonder what happened to that fabulous pocket watch he was supposed to be given from our town. As an antiques dealer, the thought of missing treasure definitely piques my interest.

Hank let out a loud snort, and pulled his head closer to his tail. Sadie gave him an affectionate smile and continued her message.

In your book you touch on some of the relationships he had in Hollywood. It seems odd to me that he never married and settled down. Did he have any children? I am enjoying your biography thoroughly and appreciate the chance to tell you so.

She signed the message and then sent it. Setting her phone on the table, she turned her attention back to her coffee and her book.

An hour later, she decided it was time to move upstairs and start settling in for bed. She let Hank outside, rinsed out her coffee cup, and then carried the Collin Malloy biography upstairs with her, Hank following at her heels.

Before she climbed into bed, she decided to check her e-mail one last time, and was surprised to see that Violet McKay had already responded.

Dear Ms. Speers,

Thank you so much for writing! I loved researching Collin Malloy and sharing his story with the world. As for the pocket watch, there are two schools of thought on that. One, that the watch was made and never delivered, and the other is that the watch was never made because the town couldn't raise enough money. At least, that's what I pieced together from old newspaper articles. I tend to believe that they just didn't raise the money because, hey, it was the Great Depression. Who could afford a diamond pocket watch? I'll scan what I've got and send it your way; I just need to dig through my files to find the articles again. I'm hard at work on a different actor's biography, so I need to haul the Malloy boxes out of storage.

As for Malloy's romantic life, there were rumors that Malloy was pretty serious about a couple of Hollywood starlets—I included their names in my book. He was too much of a bon vivant, *though, to marry. And then, of course, he died relatively young. As far as we know, he had no children.*

Thank you for your kind words. I'll scan what I've got and send it to you. It may take me several days, but I won't forget.

Cordially,

Violet McKay

Sadie read through the e-mail again, wishing it was more definite. Either Collin Malloy had a serious dalliance or he didn't. Violet McKay hadn't given her any information that she didn't already know. In fact, Sadie actually knew more than McKay did when it came to the pocket watch. Edwin had confirmed its existence through his own research, and Sadie had held it in her hands.

She fired off a quick thank-you e-mail to Violet McKay. It was nice of the author to get back to her so quickly, and nice of her to promise to share her research.

"It's time for me to start my own treasure hunt, Hank," she announced. "I need to figure out how that watch made it onto the train."

Theo opened the door to the Silver Peak Public Library, holding it open as Sara and Sadie passed through. Sadie breathed in deeply as she crossed the threshold. Nothing smelled as good as old books. In some ways, the smell of old books was better than the smell of any other kind of antique, except for perhaps the scent of old linens stored in a cedar chest.

The aroma of old books contrasted with the stark modern lines of the library building, which was a recent addition to Silver Peak. Sadie didn't count herself a fan of the building, wishing that it fit in better with the rest of the town's Victorian-era architecture, but she had grown used to it over time.

As they entered the building, Sara paused before a tall, glass-fronted case. "Hey, Grandma. Take a look."

In honor of the weeklong festivities, someone at the library had put together an exhibit of items from the 1930s. Sadie peered closer. A pair of old white leather gloves nestled against an antique autograph book, and a large, solid-looking ledger book had been flipped open, revealing two pages of fading, spidery script. What was the ledger for? Sadie inched closer and bumped her forehead against the glass.

"Hello," a voice said behind them. "Do you like our little exhibit? Anthony and I put it together."

"We do!" Sadie turned around, smiling warmly at the librarian. "Did you have these items in an archive here?"

"No." Kimama flicked one long strand of her dark hair behind her shoulder. "Most of it is borrowed from our patrons. Roz brought over the embroidered handkerchiefs." Kimama pointed at the case. "The recipe cards are from the Remingtons."

"What about this ledger?" Sadie squinted. "I can't read the writing. Is it a hotel register?"

"Actually, that's the original engineer's log from the Mountain Crest Railway," Kimama replied, a proud smile lighting her face. "Jack Fitzgerald found it in a box in his attic. It belonged to his grandfather, John Fitzgerald. He lent it to us just for this week, and then it will go on permanent display in the new station."

"How fascinating."

Sadie wished she could remove the glass barrier just so she could pore over those pages. There was nothing like an old ledger to give you a glimpse into the past. You could learn so much from the seemingly menial details inside.

Sadie reluctantly turned away from the display. "We're trying our hand at the treasure hunt that Edwin announced, so we're here to do some research on this very era in Silver Peak history. Do you know anything about Collin Malloy?"

Kimama's forehead wrinkled as she nodded slowly. "Yes, though not as much as I would like. Especially with the celebration this week."

"Yes. He was supposed to perform here one last time before going to Hollywood," Sadie replied. "For some reason, though, his last performance at the opera house was canceled. I thought we could start with the microfilm room."

"Sure thing." Kimama gestured for Sadie, Theo, and Sara to head toward the stairs. "We've got all the newspapers from that era on film, so I do hope you can find what you're looking for."

"Perfect. Thanks, Kimama."

Sadie, Theo, and Sara headed up to the second-floor microfilm room. Sadie flipped the switch on the wall as they entered the room, and waved to a bank of metal filing cabinets.

"All right, guys, each of these cabinets contains a specific newspaper," Sadie told Theo and Sara. "Back in the 1930s, there was only one daily newspaper in Silver Peak, the *Post-Gazette*. It became the *Sentinel* a decade later, so that's the one we want." She walked over to one of the filing cabinets and tugged open the top drawer.

"I remember how to work the microfilm machine." Theo proudly took his seat in front of the great, hulking machine and turned on the power switch. The reader hummed to life, its screen glowing blankly. Sara glanced at her grandmother and smiled. She and Sadie had used the machine before, together, and, while Sara loved to laugh at what she considered "ancient technology," she also knew how useful the machine could be. She crowded around the drawer with Sadie. "What date should we start with?"

Sadie looked down at the orange and white microfilm boxes. "Collin Malloy's final performance was scheduled in late May of 1931. Should we start there?"

Theo shook his head. "Let's look earlier. If the town started fund-raising before May, we'll probably find some mention of it."

Sadie nodded in approval. Theo was right. They would start with the reel containing all of May's newspapers for that year and see where they got. If they needed to go further back, they could always pick out a few more reels.

It took Theo a couple of tries to thread the film properly; the first time, he put it in upside-down, and the second time he forgot to hitch up the take-up reel. Once those problems were solved, though, he was able to whiz through the newspapers or scroll through them slowly. Sadie and Sara pulled up chairs and sat reading over his shoulder.

The Empire State Building's grand opening made headlines on the first day of that month, but there was no mention of Collin Malloy's impending trip to the opera house.

Theo moved a few pages past the first of the month. Weather reports followed advertisements. Sadie asked Theo to pause, and they stared at a department store ad.

"Wow, Grandma. You could buy a brand-new pair of pants at Werner's for two dollars."

Sadie grinned, peering at the trousers, higher waisted than anything worn now, and cut fuller in the legs too. Men's shoes cost a dollar more. Theo turned the page. A loaf of bread was ten cents.

"Crazy," Sara said.

The *Post-Gazette* was the only newspaper in town back in the 1930s, but even so, it appeared to take its mission seriously.

National and world headlines grabbed the front pages, while local news took more of a backseat. Weather reports, advertising, even classified advertisements—this was no mere village paper, but a real effort to educate and entertain readers of a small mountain community.

Sara started to fidget after about fifteen minutes. "Hey, Grandma, do you mind if I go look at that display downstairs again?"

Sadie gave her a knowing look. Sara was much more interested in getting a look at Anthony than she was in that display. "Of course. We'll find you when we're done here."

"Cool. See you guys later!" Sara left with a spring in her step, and Sadie muffled a laugh with her hand.

Theo paused, magnifying one part of the screen. Sadie scanned the section he'd highlighted and realized the *Post-Gazette* even had an entertainment section, with its own gossip column, a print version of Silver Peak's modern-day *Chatterbox* blog. Theo adjusted the screen so the gossip column grew slightly more readable. It was called *The Mother Lode* by I. C. Ahl. Sadie chuckled.

"'A certain pig got into a certain neighbor's garden,'" she read out loud. "'As they say, great fences make great neighbors. Here's hoping the Duckett family builds a dandy picket one soon.'"

They scanned the column, but it seemed to be mostly referring to events in Silver Peak, not necessarily in the world outside. There was no mention of Collin Malloy, at least not in this column.

Theo paged through the rest of the paper and on to the second day of May 1931. Theo scanned through the headlines, the local news, and the gossip columns. Nothing. They pushed on through the next several days, the microfilm reader's reels humming as Theo zipped through the pages.

They came to Wednesday, May 6, 1931. As Sadie skimmed through the columns, two words caught her eye. "Pocket Watch."

"Theo, magnify the screen, please."

Theo read the headline out loud. "Pocket Watch for Collin Malloy Engraved." They smiled at each other in satisfaction and Theo read on.

Idol of the Opera Stage to Receive Prized Gift from Denizens of Silver Peak

The diamond pocket watch for Silver Peak's favorite adopted son has been engraved by Morse and Son, Jewelers. The watch features a pavé old brilliant and rose-cut diamond case with a rose-cut diamond loop for suspension. The jeweler confirms that the watch features a jeweled movement by the well-known Elgin National Watch Company. The case has been engraved in script, reading:

To Our Adopted Son, Collin Malloy

From the Citizens of Silver Peak

The entire community has rallied together to provide Mr. Malloy with this tribute at his final performance for the Silver Peak Opera House, raising nearly one thousand dollars to purchase the watch and engraving.

At this final performance, Mr. Malloy will be singing well-known favorites, including his roles from Puccini, Verdi, and Bellini. The show is schedule for 22 May at seven o'clock in the evening.

There, at the bottom of the column, was a grainy, blurry picture of a diamond pocket watch.

"Aha!" Theo pressed the "Print Screen" button.

Sadie beamed at her grandson's enthusiasm and leaned forward to study the photo.

That was the watch. She had only held it for a moment, but she would recognize that particular piece of jewelry anywhere.

11

Now they had the date for Collin Malloy's farewell concert and a picture of the pocket watch.

The microfilm reader printed out the data on the screen with a great deal of shuddering and beeping. When the printer spit out the picture, it was a negative of what they had seen on the screen, and a very blurry negative at that.

"Better than nothing, I guess." Theo handed Sadie the picture.

Sara came back into the microfilm room.

"Hey, Sara. We found the watch!" Theo said.

Sara gasped. "For real? You know where it is?"

Sadie shook her head. "No, we just found a picture of it. But we know now what it looks like." She held the picture out to Sara, who studied it with interest.

"Cool. I bet it's worth a fortune."

"Definitely, but it's also worth a lot to our town's history." Sadie folded the picture and stuffed it into her purse.

Sara stretched her arms above her head. "So are we done? I'm starved. Can we go to Los Pollitos?"

Sadie glanced down at her watch. She'd set a late afternoon coffee date with Roz over a week ago, and if she didn't leave soon, she'd be late. "I'm going to have coffee with Roz, but you two can go on without me."

"Great!" Sara headed for the door. "I want a burrito."

"A taco plate sounds good to me." Theo turned off the microfilm machine.

When they got downstairs, Theo and Sara hugged Sadie and headed off for their afternoon snack. Sadie couldn't blame them. If she could still eat like a teenager, she'd be up for a burrito right now too. The food at Los Pollitos was just so good.

Kimama was working at the circulation desk up front, stamping a pile of books that teetered precariously close to the edge of the table.

"Kimama," Sadie called as she walked toward her. "Is it okay if I leave the reader set up as it is? I have a coffee date but I plan to come back in an hour or so."

"That should be fine." Kimama gave her a brisk smile as she continued her work. "It's usually pretty quiet on Tuesday afternoons, but if anyone needs the machine, I can reset it for them."

"Thanks. See you in a bit!"

Sadie walked out the front doors, heading toward Arbuckle's. As she strolled down the sidewalk, the late afternoon sun warming her face, she resisted the urge to pull the article back out of her purse to study the picture of the watch.

Roz had commandeered a table near the window of Arbuckle's and smiled and waved as Sadie caught her eye. Sadie grinned and hurried into the coffee shop, where Roz enveloped her in a warm hug as though they hadn't seen each other in weeks.

"Sadie! Guess what," Roz murmured in her ear. "I just saw the elusive Mr. Natty Flats!" She gave a theatrical shiver as if she'd seen the Loch Ness monster instead.

"Now, Roz!" Sadie chided her friend gently. Natty had been an enigmatic, peculiar figure around Silver Peak even when Roz and Sadie were growing up there. As children, they had been a little afraid of the stern, hawkish-looking older man and had often run away when they saw him coming. But as an adult, Sadie saw him for what he really was: a dignified elderly man worthy of respect, whose years of living alone in the mountains had stripped him of all but the barest of social graces. Intensely private, yet known for his flashy, formal attire, the man seldom came down from his house high above Silver Peak, so a sighting of the eccentric man was indeed rare.

"You know what I mean, Sadie," Roz said. "That man is as peculiar as they come."

"I've seen him too, actually—a couple of times recently." Sadie tugged her arms out of her polar fleece jacket and dropped it over the back of her chair. "I wonder why he's been coming to town."

"He definitely looked like a man on a mission." Roz sat, her coffee cup in her hands. "I saw him heading toward the edge of town."

"I saw him in the pawn shop yesterday." A rising sense of curiosity welled within Sadie. Natty had appeared in town for several days now. "Whatever it is, it has to be a big deal."

Roz had thoughtfully ordered ahead, and selected something more adventurous than Sadie might have tried on her own: a chai latte. Sadie took a careful sip, finding that she liked the rich, sweet blend of spices. "How much do I owe you?"

Roz brushed away her question with a sweep of her hand. "It's my treat this time, Sadie."

"Oh, thanks. I'll get you next time."

Roz took a sip of her drink, then smiled. "So tell me what you've been up to." She propped her elbows on the table and fixed Sadie with that familiar, knowing look. Sadie couldn't keep secrets from Roz for long—Roz knew her too well. The look she was giving Sadie now was the same look she gave her in kindergarten, when Sadie received a certificate for being a good citizen and was bursting at the seams to tell someone.

Sadie tilted her chin and eyed her friend impishly. "I don't know where to begin. Since the train ride, so much has happened!"

Roz dropped her chin into her hands, her eyes widening. "Well, don't keep me in suspense!"

In between sips of her chai latte, Sadie regaled Roz with the week's events, working backward from Grace Elliott's after-hours earring hunt to finding Collin Malloy's pocket watch and holding it in her hand.

"See, here it is." Sadie rummaged around in her purse and brought out the printout of the newspaper article. "That's the watch I found that night. How on earth did it get onto the train, and how did it stay there that long?"

Roz leaned toward her, eyes wide. "I think the more important question is, did you drop it, or was it taken from you?"

Sadie sighed, folding the newspaper article back up in a neat square. "I think it was taken from me, but if so, the person who took it managed to get it out of my hand without my noticing. One minute it was there. The next—*poof!*—it was gone."

Roz nodded thoughtfully. "I see what you mean. Even then, it just doesn't make sense. I mean, who would know it was on the train in the first place? It's too bad there's no one to ask. Most everyone who was alive during that time has passed away, though."

"Almost everyone." Sadie set her coffee cup aside, a thought forming in her mind. "But what about Natty? He might remember. I could talk to him."

"Talk to Natty Flats?" Roz's eyes widened.

"Why not?" Sadie was getting more excited about this idea the more she thought about it. "Natty was a child back in the 1930s, but he remembers the train. He remembers the rail yard. He told me so. I wonder if he could recall anything further if I asked him."

"Well, good luck." Roz's eyebrows drew together as she contemplated her cup. She looked at Sadie quizzically. "Tell me, though. If you had to guess who you think did it, what would your guess be and why?"

"My seatmate disappearing the way he did was very suspicious, and he was right there when I fell." Sadie sighed. "But I still don't know for sure. He spoke to Darcy Burke, who also vanished the very next day. Maybe they worked together?"

"If you ask me, the Elliotts seem pretty suspicious. It sounds like they could use the money they'd get from a watch like that. And they were on the train near you." Roz folded her napkin and put it to one side. "Shall we order dessert?"

Sadie consulted her watch. The afternoon was waning quickly. If she wanted to get more research done, she'd better rush back to the library. "No, thanks. Not this time. I need to get back to work."

Sadie stood and put on her coat. "I'd love to be able to find the watch once more. It would look so fabulous on display in the station. Just think what it would mean for the town!"

Roz smiled up at her. "If anyone can find it, you can."

Sadie hugged Roz good-bye and hustled back to the library.

As she walked in, Kimama glanced up from her position at the circulation desk. "Back already?"

"Oh, you know me. I love my research." Sadie paused in front of the display case once more. "Do you have any other material relating to the Mountain Crest Railway? Besides this engineer's log, I mean."

"Sara asked about that too. We have a menu from the dining car, and the ashtray you see there was in the original passenger car," Kimama replied. "But all the records for the railway were destroyed in a fire back in the 1950s. There's hardly anything left. It's actually surprising that we found as much as we did."

"That's too bad." Lost and destroyed records weren't at all that uncommon, but it never failed to disappoint Sadie. "Well, back to the salt mines."

Kimama smiled. "In Silver Peak? You'd better say back to the silver mines."

Sadie made a mental note, as she walked back into the microfilm room, to ask if she could examine the items in the display case. They might yield something interesting, and at the very least, it would be fun to hold them up close.

She turned the microfilm reader on again and paged through the rest of May 1931.

Once the initial announcement of the watch had been made, it popped up a few times here and there throughout the month.

According to one article, the newspapers in Denver had picked up the story too. *The Mother Lode* gossip column mentioned, a week before the concert, that Malloy had been offered a screen test and potential film contract with Global Pictures, one of the biggest film studios in Hollywood. According to the item, Malloy's screen test was scheduled for a week after his last concert.

Sadie skipped ahead to May 22. There, on the front page, was a picture of Collin Malloy that she had seen in Violet McKay's book, one with Malloy in a tuxedo and top hat. Beside it, the *Post-Gazette* had included another picture of the pocket watch. The headline read:

LOCAL HERO TO PERFORM TONIGHT
Malloy's farewell concert sold out

The article didn't provide much new information, but it did state that the pocket watch was to be delivered to the opera house from the jeweler that morning, and that the presentation of the watch would be after Malloy's final solo.

Sadie chewed her bottom lip and pressed the print screen button. A copy of the article sputtered and whirred out of the machine, hitting the floor.

She moved to the next day. Surely there would be some kind of news, some kind of announcement. If Malloy had broken such a widely anticipated engagement, there would be tickets to repay if nothing else.

All she found was a tiny paragraph buried in the back of the entertainment page. "Collin Malloy Heads to Hollywood."

The residents of Silver Peak wish to extend our heartiest of congratulations to Mr. Malloy, who left town yesterday to pursue his screen test with Global Pictures. Mr. Malloy's screen test was suddenly pressed forward by studio executives, and we hope that their eagerness is a portent of Malloy's box-office draw.

That was it. No explanation beyond the sudden need for Global Pictures to test him immediately. Nothing about ticket refunds or whether Malloy had ever made it to the opera house before leaving Colorado for California.

Something about this sudden quiet made Sadie pause. She wondered if Silver Peak had experienced a collective round of hurt feelings and decided never to speak of the matter again. Or perhaps this sudden silence indicated something even deeper. A conspiracy to stay quiet for some reason? If so, why?

Sadie paged through the rest of 1931, but no mention of Collin Malloy appeared again. Malloy went on to enjoy great fame and fortune before his untimely death. Why didn't Silver Peak brag about it? There had to be something behind this sudden hush.

She pushed forward, glancing through 1932 and finally reaching the end of 1933, but nothing further mentioning Collin Malloy appeared.

With a sigh, Sadie hit the rewind button and the film slowly began the process of moving from the take-up reel to its storage reel. As images and words flashed past, one sentence caught her eye.

Sadie paused the machine and flicked forward, looking for that elusive mention. December 13, 1933, a brief blurb in the *Mother Lode.*

Collin Malloy, Global Pictures' featured player and movie musical star, is said to be twinkling with another star. Or in this case, a starlet who shines brightly.

That was it. Nothing too exciting. After all, Violet McKay mentioned Malloy's popularity with the leading ladies in her book. Even so, Sadie pressed the print screen button. If nothing else, this was of interest because it appeared to be the last time Collin Malloy was mentioned by the town that had loved him so fiercely. It was a disappointing tribute, but she should keep it just the same.

Sadie wound the microfilm and put it away, keeping the room as orderly as she used to keep her own classroom back in her teaching days. Then she turned off the light.

She waved good-bye to Kimama and headed back to check on Julie at the Antique Mine, her mind full of questions. Should she really speak to Natty? Primary source research was only getting them so far. Talking to people who lived in the era was really the ideal way to find out more.

Besides, Natty was an interesting character. He probably had a lot of stories to tell, if she could get him to open up to her.

12

Sadie set her travel coffee mug on the counter and opened the register. Another morning at the Antique Mine, and Julie would be in later today. As she counted out the change into the cash drawer, she glanced down at a morning paper from Denver. Sadie closed the drawer and settled down at the desk to read the news while the store was still quiet.

As she paged through the newspaper, one headline in the business section grabbed her attention:

POSSIBLE LEVERAGED BUYOUT TO SAVE ELLIOTT ENVIRONMENTAL SOFTWARE

Thomas Elliott pronounces Japanese company a "good partner in the fight."

Next to the article was a professional headshot of Grace Elliott's husband.

Sadie grabbed the paper, holding it closer so she could read the article. The Elliotts' financial trouble had been serious, Sadie realized. Apparently, Mr. Elliott had commingled his personal funds with his business funds, and that made him personally liable when his business began to fail. She sat back for a moment, considering the matter. That meant when Elliott Environmental

Software looked like it was going to face bankruptcy, the Elliotts themselves could have been held accountable for their company's debts.

None of that really explained why Grace Elliott had been so determined to find her lost earring. Sadie remembered her conversation with Joe. Was it possible that Grace had used that very earring to commit some kind of insurance fraud?

That kind of payout could help save them from bankruptcy, perhaps, or at the very least it could help mitigate the amount of cash they'd have to come up with. Desperate times could definitely call for desperate measures, but would it lead to fraud and theft?

It depended on the character of the people in desperate times, Sadie mused. The Elliotts had been on the train during its inaugural run. Would their situation compel them to orchestrate the theft of Collin Malloy's valuable diamond pocket watch? It was possible. But a bit of a stretch. After all, how would the Elliotts have known the watch was on the train?

Sadie put her coffee cup down and resumed reading.

The Japanese company in question was planning to announce the buyout by the end of the week, and by all accounts, it looked like Thomas Elliott would be put in charge of the United States division of the newly formed corporation.

Sadie was roused from her contemplations by a loud, percussive *thump* across the street. She jumped, grabbed her coffee mug, and hurried to the front of the store. She opened the door and stepped outside, shielding her eyes against the sun's glare.

Another loud *thump* signaled the presence of a roofing crew atop Spike's music shop. Ardis Fleagle must have had an opening in his schedule to have started on Spike's shop already. She had hoped they'd wait until after this week's festivities. After all, installing a new roof was loud and messy work, and all the shop owners wanted to attract customers—not drive them away with noise and dust.

Sadie watched as the men worked, her emotions torn. On the one hand, it was great that Spike was fixing the roof. On the other hand, it was potentially disastrous for business this week.

Ardis spotted her from across the street and waved. He jogged over, clipboard in hand and hard hat tilted back on his head. "Hi, Sadie!" he called as he got close.

"Hi, Ardis." Sadie shook his hand warmly. "How long do you think the job will take? I know mine was done more quickly than I expected."

Ardis shook his head. "It's going to take longer than yours. We're going to have to replace some of the roof deck. It's rotted through."

Sadie's eyes widened. That sounded expensive. "Goodness. I guess that's what insurance is for, though."

"Nah, insurance won't cover this." Ardis squinted at his clipboard, then looked up at Sadie and grinned. "So I bet you're participating in this treasure hunt, being the Antique Lady. I'm looking under every roof for treasure."

Sadie nodded. Ardis probably saw all kinds of things stashed under rooflines, or even in chimneys and walls. "My grandchildren and I did some research yesterday, but we haven't decided where to search yet."

Ardis turned sharply at another loud *thud* and peered up at his crew. "'Scuse me, Sadie, but I gotta run. If I don't keep a watch on some of these guys, they're liable to drop a hammer on someone."

Sadie walked back inside the Antique Mine, the clanging noise from the crew echoing throughout the store. Poor Spike. Having his roof rebuilt would be expensive, and if his insurance wouldn't help, he'd be stuck with the bill. If the roof was damaged and leaking, though, he didn't have a choice. He'd have to pay for the repairs, because leaving the roof to rot would cause far more problems in the long run.

She wandered around the store, changing displays and rearranging items in the cases. It was time for a change. Maybe she'd have Julie work on some new displays when she came in this afternoon. Julie had such a flair for décor.

Sadie returned to her place behind the counter, and the box of movie stills caught her eye. She'd nearly forgotten about them. She'd pulled them out of the back room to help her make her Collin Malloy display, but she hadn't unpacked or priced the rest of them since choosing the photos she wanted to hang on the wall.

Sadie set to work sorting the photos into piles of movie stills, portrait stills, and candid shots. Then she found an old Shaker basket and propped the stills up inside so that customers could flip through them without having to take them all out and sort through the pile.

Sadie stepped back to look at her handiwork and decided she'd ask Julie to create dividers and a sign for the basket. It would look much prettier when Julie finished with it.

"Looks good," a familiar voice boomed in her ear.

Sadie jumped, spinning around.

Edwin gave her a boyish smile and held out a cup of coffee from Arbuckle's. "Midmorning treat," he said loudly. He nodded toward Spike's shop. "How on earth can you stand the noise?"

"I'm afraid it will affect business." Sadie gratefully accepted the coffee cup. "Here. Let's sit back in the corner. I hope the noise won't be so bad and I can still keep an eye on the shop."

Edwin picked up the brown bag he'd set on the counter and followed her to the back corner, expertly weaving in and out of the crowded aisles. Sadie set her coffee cup down on a small table and tugged two rocking chairs together, angling them so they pointed out into the store. The roofing noise was more of a dull roar back here, so they would be able to talk without having to shout.

Edwin pulled a blueberry muffin out of the bag. "I felt bad about missing two dinners with you, so I thought it would be nice if we could have a morning break together."

Sadie's heart glowed as she took the muffin. "How sweet, Edwin. Thank you."

"I found a judge to replace the one who is sick, and the rest of the events have been humming along just fine." Edwin sat in the rocking chair opposite her, and took a drink from his coffee cup. "How has your week been?"

"Pretty exciting, actually." Sadie smiled. "Theo, Sara, and I found a picture of the pocket watch, and it is definitely the one I found on the train."

Edwin paused midsip, glancing at her over the rim of his coffee cup before speaking. "Well, I guess it's good to have that confirmed. What else have you learned?"

She told him about everything else she'd been up to, between enjoyable sips of coffee and delicious bites of blueberry muffin. She loved coffee no matter what the variety, but Arbuckle's dark roasts were definitely her favorite.

"So what are you going to do next, now that you know the watch is the one you found on the train?" Edwin sat back in his chair, eyeing her expectantly.

"I'm going to talk to Natty Flats." She polished off the last bit of muffin, wadding up the paper wrapper into a ball. "He was around back then. There aren't many people left who were. He might have heard something about the watch. Maybe he can point us in the right direction." She smiled at him. "I'm excited about talking to him, actually. Natty must know a lot about Silver Peak. I bet he's a treasure trove of information."

Edwin shook his head. "I'm not sure that's such a great idea, Sadie."

"Why not?" Despite herself, Sadie felt a little ruffled. She tossed the blueberry wrapper into the bag, purposely avoiding Edwin's gaze. "Are you worried that he's dangerous?" Her conversation with Roz flitted through her mind.

"No, Sadie. I am not worried that Natty is dangerous." Edwin's voice grew softer. "I'm just not sure he'll be in the mood to chat."

Sadie paused, studying Edwin. "You know why he's in town."

Edwin sighed. "Yesterday I saw him hanging around at City Hall, but he couldn't get anywhere with the clerks, so I invited him up to my office. We talked for half an hour."

The annoyance that had briefly flared within Sadie died away. Edwin's posture and gaze told her that he was absolutely serious—that the situation as a whole was grave. "Is he okay? What's going on?"

Edwin shook his head. "I can't give you details, but he's in danger of losing everything he has. I wish I could help, but I don't know what to do about it."

"We'll find some way to help him. I know we can." Sadie's heart surged. Surely the whole community could find a way to support Natty.

"I've even spoken to see if they have room for Natty at the state hospital," Edwin admitted. "At least, when that time comes. He's remarkably healthy for his age, but what if he falls while he's up in that cabin by himself? If he's in a hospital, he'll be fed and taken care of."

Sadie shook her head. "Oh, Edwin, keep that as a last resort. Natty is a part of Silver Peak. We owe it to him to find a way to keep him here as long as we can."

"I appreciate your thoughts, Sadie, but please don't say anything to anyone else or start trying to raise support." Edwin covered her hand with his. "Natty would be offended and possibly even hurt if he knew I told you. I could tell it took so much for him to come and ask me for help. I don't want you to interview him, because I know he's dealing with a lot of difficult situations right now. We should respect his privacy."

She nodded and sat quietly with Edwin as the din from the roofers rumbled dully in the background. Edwin was wise and was trying to help Natty. If she continued to argue her point with him, it would spoil the first moments they'd had together in days.

She hadn't given up the idea of talking to Natty Flats, though. He might be her best chance of finding out how that pocket watch made it onto that train.

13

That afternoon, after Julie arrived to take over the shop, Sadie, Theo, and Sara walked to the library. After all, they'd had good luck by doing primary research so far. Why not dig around for more information? There was always the possibility that one of them could unearth another treasure trove.

Kimama smiled from the circulation desk as she pushed open the heavy glass door. "Welcome back! What'll it be today?"

Sadie chuckled. "We'll start with your exhibit, I think." Sadie peered through the glass at the engineer's log. "What year is this ledger from?"

"It runs from 1930 to 1931."

"Really? That's perfect!" Sadie turned to the librarian. "Can we take a closer look at it?"

"Of course. You know I would trust you with anything we have on display."

Kimama pulled the keys to the case from her pocket and unlocked it with swift efficiency. The three of them followed her to a back room, Kimama walking so straight and so softly that her long hair barely swished against her back.

Kimama placed the log on a long, low oaken table. "Normally I'd make you use gloves to handle this, but these pages are so fragile that I think wearing gloves would make it more difficult to turn the pages and thus more likely to tear them."

Sadie nodded. "We'll be extracareful."

Kimama gave her a trusting smile and left the room.

Sara and Theo pulled up chairs closer to the table, as Sadie began reading the logbook. Page after page was filled with John Fitzgerald's precise handwriting.

"The entries show the same basic details every day—departure times, arrival times, and the weather." Theo scooted his chair a little closer.

"I suppose the engineer was mostly interested in keeping his train running on time."

"So what was the weather like the day Collin Malloy came to town?" Sara wondered.

"Let's find out." Sadie carefully turned the pages until she came to May 22, 1931.

She had to turn this particular page with extra care, as it was splattered with ink that made the fragile paper stick to itself. She gently pried the pages apart and smoothed them out so they could read the entries.

"'May 22, 1931. Moved...*...west. 13C. Time will tell,'" Theo read out loud, pronouncing the word *asterisk* for the symbol. He glanced down at the bottom of the page, as if seeking a footnote, then glanced up to meet Sadie's eyes with a shake of his head.

"Well, that's different." Sadie shook her head. "I wonder if there are any other entries like this one."

Sara leaned forward, propping her elbows on the table. "What's all over the page? Is it ink?"

"Yes." Sadie gently rubbed her fingertip over the dried ink. "He must have written this in a hurry to splatter it all over the page like this. Probably using a fountain pen and not stopping to blot it. His other entries are very neat and precise."

"'Moved * west.'" Theo read once more. "Do you think it's his cargo? He hasn't mentioned what freight he was carrying before."

Sadie nodded. "He was the engineer of a passenger train, so there was no freight to record. He was moving people, not goods." She stared at the entry as a jolt of excitement hit her. *People, not goods.*

Theo must have had the same thought, as his eyes met hers with an excited flash of recognition. "Asterisk...Star! Collin Malloy?"

Sara straightened. "Oh yeah! That must be it!"

"Wow. Pretty cryptic. What about 'west'?" Theo asked.

"Well, Malloy had a Hollywood screen test later that same month," Sadie said. "He probably took the train west to pursue his Tinseltown dreams."

"Yep. It could be west to California." Theo's eyes glowed with interest. "So what about '13C'?"

They all stared at the words. Where had Sadie seen this exact reference before? The image of a brass plate with Art Deco lettering flashed across her mind.

"Of course! My seat on the train was in row 13, seat C—a window seat."

Had Collin Malloy sat in that very seat when he left Silver Peak for the last time? Sadie frowned. But then, how did the watch come to be hidden there? Had it fallen out of Malloy's pocket?

That would mean he'd received it after all. But if that was the case, why didn't the newspaper feature any articles about the presentation? Why did town history claim that Malloy was never given the watch?

"What about the next part, Grandma?" Sara asked.

"'Time will tell.'" Sadie sighed. "I have no idea what it could mean, unless the engineer was referring to Malloy's hopes for stardom."

"That seems kind of odd. I mean, why would he care?" Theo leaned back in his chair.

"Why would he take the time to jot down a note about a passenger at all, when he only noted the most basic facts and data in his logbook?" Sadie frowned. "And why make it so secretive?" This felt like valuable information, if only they could decipher its meaning.

Sara pulled her phone out of her pocket. "Can I take a picture of it?"

"Good idea." Sadie patted her granddaughter's arm. "Just make sure you turn off your flash." After all, a camera's flash was as bright as the light from a photocopier, and after handling rare and brittle books over the years, Sadie knew that some objects just couldn't be exposed to routine research treatment.

"Sure." Sara tapped her phone screen a couple of times, then held it above the ledger, moving it up and down and angling it until she was happy with the shot. The phone made two shutter sounds, then Sara sat back in her chair, satisfied. She turned the phone to show the photo to Sadie and Theo.

"Maybe it's time to ask another expert," Sadie said. "I've been e-mailing a biographer named Violet McKay, who wrote a book about Collin Malloy. Maybe she can help us out."

She pulled up her e-mail in-box on her phone and composed a note to Violet McKay, using its small on-screen keyboard.

Dear Ms. McKay,

Sorry to bother you again, but we are researching Collin Malloy's time in Silver Peak and are very curious about his relationship with the townspeople. In your book you mention that Malloy was often mobbed by fans. Do you know if he had any situations like that here in Silver Peak? Were his relationships here mostly good? Do you know if he was particularly close with anyone (or perhaps had any enemies)? Why, in your opinion, was he so fond of our little town? Any information you have will be most appreciated.

Thank you!

Sadie Speers

Sadie read the message out loud to her grandchildren, and they nodded in approval.

"If he had crazed fans lurking here, that could explain this entry. Maybe he had to sneak out of town." Sadie stretched and yawned. She was beginning to cramp up from sitting too close to the logbook.

Even though Sara had photos of the ledger, Sadie decided to write the entry for herself. She pulled her notebook from her purse, scribbled the cryptic entry on a fresh page, and then tucked the journal back into her bag.

"Grandma, we should probably leave soon." Theo's tone sounded reluctant as he glanced at his phone. "The library's going to close in half an hour."

"Before we go, let's page through the rest of the 1931 entries and see if anything else unusual leaps out at us."

Sadie turned the next delicate page over gently, and all three of them stared down at the ledger.

The next page held only two entries—for May 28 and May 29—and then ended. The rest of the ledger was blank.

"What happened?" Sara asked.

"Maybe he started a new ledger," Theo said. Then he frowned. "But he ended this one before the end of the month, and there are so many extra pages left. That doesn't make sense."

Sara's eyes widened. "Do you think something happened? Did he lose his job?"

Sadie stared at the last entry in the ledger, waiting for it to provide some clue, but it didn't. Like all of the other entries in the ledger, it stated weather, departure time, and arrival time.

And then nothing.

"I don't know," she said. "We'll have to do some more research to find out what happened."

Sara groaned and jumped out of her chair. "This mystery just keeps getting more... mysterious."

Sadie chuckled. "Well, whatever happened to the engineer to make him quit this ledger, May 22 must have been an important day." Theo carefully picked up the logbook. "It was such a big deal that this guy broke his routine."

Theo was right. Something big had happened that day—but what could it be?

Sadie arrived home that evening just as her housekeeper, Claribel, was leaving. Sadie waved to her as their cars passed each other on the long driveway, and Claribel waved back with a big smile.

Once she was inside, Sadie let Hank out to run around while her computer booted up. While he frisked about on the front lawn, she watched him out the window until her Internet browser opened and she could access her e-mail account.

Violet McKay had already responded to her e-mail. *Wow, that was fast.* Sadie opened the message, her fingers trembling a little in anticipation.

Hi, Ms. Speers!

Funny you should mention it. As I was going through my files on Collin Malloy, I found some more information on his relationship with Silver Peak. I didn't really use it in my book, and I forgot all about it, since my focus was primarily on his career. But I thought maybe you'd be interested. It appears that Malloy was good friends with a train engineer named John Fitzgerald. It was this man who brought Malloy to Silver Peak for the first time and fostered Malloy's love for the town and its citizens.

I scanned the articles and attached them to this message.

If there's anything more I can do to help, feel free to ask.

Violet

Sadie found the information about John Fitzgerald and Malloy intriguing—and useful. Their friendship could account for the special entry in the engineer's ledger.

The author had attached three files. Sadie opened the first one, a newspaper clipping that proclaimed in a bold headline "Collin Malloy Recalls Poor Irish Roots."

The article was not dated, but obviously had been written after Malloy achieved some measure of success and fame in

Hollywood. It was an interview with the actor in which he talked about his early days of running barefoot through working-class streets of northeast Denver. The reporter was obviously enamored with Malloy's background and his quick rise to fame. About halfway through the article, Sadie paused, rereading the paragraph through a few times.

"I had some high times with my old buddy, John Fitzgerald. John and I grew up as a couple of wild hooligans, but I guess we did all right by ourselves in the end. John helped me get my big break, you know. From his early days hopping freight trains, he became a legitimate engineer on a railway. His trips into Silver Peak introduced him to the folks there, and he learned they had an opera house. I was so broke then, so I followed John to Silver Peak one night and literally sang for my supper. The kind people I met there really gave me my start."

Sadie sat back in her chair for a moment. She felt certain that this friendship had continued throughout Malloy's stay in Silver Peak and that, somehow, John Fitzgerald had been involved with Collin Malloy's last performance—or lack thereof. Whatever had occurred had been important enough that John made a note in his log, where he usually recorded the mere facts of his job. It was all tied together somehow—May 22, seat 13C, the pocket watch. She was so close to knowing what had happened all those years ago.

Sadie double-clicked on the other two attachments. These last two articles seemed to be more along the lines of gossip column fragments. She zoomed in on the faded, blurred typewritten copy.

One merely stated "Collin Malloy seen at the Coconut Grove with his *du jour*, costar Margaret Malone." The fragment was undated. Obviously during his Hollywood career, but at what point in his climb to fame?

The other attachment was also a gossip column, but this one was dated June 6, 1933, about six months before Malloy passed away. The column ran to about five paragraphs, and Sadie scanned them quickly.

Betty Bright, of Global Pictures fame, is taking the next two months off to recover from an appendectomy. Miss Bright fell ill while vacationing in Hawaii with her mother. We all wish her the speediest of recoveries.

Sadie smiled. Betty Bright was the young starlet she had discovered while making her Collin Malloy display at the Antique Mine. It was fun to see her name in a gossip column, even if it was for something as distressing as surgery. Sadie skipped ahead until she found a mention of Malloy.

Collin Malloy, the tenor whom every girl in Hollywood dreams of, has just signed a six-picture deal with Epic Pictures. No official word on the great man's salary yet, but we have every reason to believe that Margaret Malone can someday plan to feather their love nest—with sables.

So Margaret Malone—another actress in her Malloy display—seemed to be a permanent fixture of Malloy's romantic life at this point. At least they were enough of an "item" that Hollywood columnists were speculating openly about their relationship.

Robert Smith's face flashed across Sadie's memory, and she wondered briefly how serious Collin Malloy's romantic involvement with Margaret Malone really was.

Sadie dashed off a quick e-mail to Violet McKay, thanking her for sending the information. Then she let Hank back in, patting his smooth, glossy coat as he trotted by.

Now that she had the Fitzgerald connection, it was time to figure out more about that cryptic log entry.

Her phone buzzed with a text. It was from Sara.

Hey, Grandma, I want to enter the essay contest. I want to write about how we're doing research for the treasure hunt. Also I want to write about what the watch means for our town.

Sadie smiled, surprised that Sara was so interested in the treasure hunt. Or maybe she just wanted the Sophia's gift certificate meant for the winner.

Go for it, she texted back. Her phone buzzed again.

Mom thinks it would help if I could talk to someone from that era. Sara messaged back. *Can you help?*

That would help Sadie as well. Sadie could think of only one candidate. He had been a boy in the thirties, and had even played around the rail yards. He, of anyone in Silver Peak, would be most likely to remember John Fitzgerald or have heard tales about Collin Malloy's diamond pocket watch. Edwin was worried that Natty had too much on his mind to want to talk to her, but Sadie thought it was just as possible that reminiscing might be comforting. It certainly wouldn't hurt to ask, at least.

It was time to seek out Mr. Natty Flats.

14

Of course, deciding to talk to Natty Flats was one thing.

Finding him was quite another.

Natty had demonstrated an uncanny way of appearing and disappearing in town, and unless she sought him out in his mountain cabin, she wasn't sure where to start looking for him. She decided to let Edwin know what she was up to, just in case her search took her off the beaten path, but also because of their earlier discussion.

As mayor of Silver Peak, Edwin was in the thick of the town festival activities, so she was reluctant to call and interrupt him. But after his caution about Natty's fragile financial circumstances, she felt Edwin might need to be reassured that she would proceed delicately. She speed-dialed his cell phone number, fully expecting it to go into voice mail.

"Well, just the person I hoped to hear from," Edwin's resonant voice boomed in her ear.

"Oh?" Sadie said with a laugh. "What did I do now?"

Edwin chuckled. "Nothing. I just wanted to hear the sound of your voice."

Sadie's heart warmed. "Well, it's great to hear yours too. I figured I'd get your voice mail. How's everything at the festivities?"

Sadie could picture him, standing near Silver Peak's Paseo River, where vendors and organizations had set up tents and booths, and food trucks were doling out every kind of food imaginable.

He laughed. "It's going well, but I'll be glad when my shift is over, and I can head back to the quiet of my office for a while."

"I can understand that," Sadie said. "I won't keep you, but I wanted to let you know what I'm up to here."

She went on to tell him of her plans to find Natty Flats. After a moment of silence, punctuated by sounds of the festival activities around him, he said, "Of course I trust you to tread lightly with Natty."

"I will." Sadie could hear voices in the background, and Edwin added, "Okay, Sadie. Some folks are stopping by. Talk to you later."

They said their good-byes and ended the call.

She wasn't sure if she wanted to venture into the mountains to track Natty down yet. She knew approximately where his small cabin was situated, but since she had seen him so many times recently, it might make more sense to seek him out around Silver Peak. She left Julie in charge of the shop all morning and drove and walked around town, looking for Natty, asking around if people had seen him, but her search was fruitless.

She returned to the shop after lunch in need of a better plan. During an afternoon lull, Sadie decided that if she couldn't track down Natty Flats, she could try to track down some other leads.

She picked up her phone and dialed Jack Fitzgerald's office at the train station. When that went to voice mail, she debated a moment, and then decided to try his cell phone.

"Hello?"

"Hi, Jack, it's Sadie."

"Sadie, hi. I'm afraid we haven't found your missing antiques yet." She could hear some loud music and a lot of voices in the background. "I've gotten into two separate arguments with the cleaners and interviewed every one of my staff, but no one has any idea what happened to them."

Hmm. Maybe they'd been stolen after all.

"Thanks for the effort, Jack, I appreciate it."

"We'll pay for them, Sadie. Just tell me how much I owe you."

"Let's give it a few more days. You might still figure out where they went."

"Okay, if you're sure. Was that it? I'm at my niece's wedding reception right now."

"Oh, I'm so sorry to disturb you! Is this Darcy's wedding? Please pass on my congratulations!"

"Yeah, sure. I will."

Sadie thought about her missing antiques and about how Darcy had quit just after they disappeared. "Has she told you why she quit?"

Jack sighed again. "That girl! She claims she needed time to prepare for her wedding, but she didn't have to quit for that. I would have given her time off, of course. But she won't talk to me about it. She's just as stubborn as her father."

Sadie laughed. "Well, maybe you can coax her back after the honeymoon."

"Yeah, maybe."

Sadie sat down behind the shop's counter. "I actually had a completely different question for you, about your grandfather."

"Oh?" Jack's tone brightened several notches. "What about him?"

"Kimama let me examine that wonderful ledger you lent to the library, and I noticed that it ended rather abruptly, with several empty pages. I just wondered what happened, if anything."

Jack sighed. "Last entry, May 29, 1933? My grandfather died that very night, of a heart attack. It was a shock to everyone, because he was still fairly young and seemed healthy. May 29 was his last day of work."

"Oh, Jack, I'm so sorry to hear that."

"Well, I never knew him, of course, but my grandmother loved him until the day she died and told us stories about him all the time." He laughed and added, "Whether we wanted to hear them or not!"

"Well, thanks for sharing that with me. That ledger must be truly precious to your family."

"It is. I can't wait to put it on display here at the station so his legacy lives on. Too bad my grandmother isn't here to see it."

Sadie smiled. "It'll be wonderful. Thanks, Jack, I'll let you get back to the reception. Have fun!"

"Thanks, Sadie."

"Bye!"

Sadie hung up and stared absently at her Collin Malloy display for several minutes, thinking. John Fitzgerald had been close to Malloy and had, according to his cryptic log entry, possibly helped Malloy sneak out of town. And then a short time later he had died. She wondered how much of the mystery surrounding Malloy's final departure from Silver Peak had gone to the grave with John Fitzgerald.

Later that afternoon, as Sadie began closing the Antique Mine and turned over the sign on the door to read Closed, she glanced across the street at Spike's shop. The roofers had already packed up for the evening, and as both the dusk and the dust settled, she could just pick out a light glowing in his apartment.

She totaled her receipts for the day and sighed at the final number. The noise and activity surrounding Spike's roof had definitely put a dent in sales today.

Sadie flicked off the last of the lights and opened the door. As she stepped outside, a hunched figure with a familiar loping stride scuttled toward the corner.

"Mr. Flats?"

The man paused, only the bottom half of his face visible beneath the brim of his fedora. He lifted the hat and nodded. "Sadie Speers."

Sadie swallowed and pressed herself forward. She had absolutely no idea how to start this conversation. "It's nice to see you around town."

"Is it." It was a statement, not a question, and Natty seemed poised for flight.

"Yes, sir." Sadie again recalled Edwin's concern about Natty's poverty. Perhaps she could offer him something to eat. "Could I treat you to some enchiladas at Los Pollitos tonight? I'm too tired to go home and cook and it would be nice to have company."

Natty raised his head. "Can't have enchiladas. The chili con carne gives me a misery in my stomach."

"Well, perhaps we could order something else." Sadie gave him an understanding smile. "I know they make a really good chicken tortilla soup. It's pretty mild too."

Natty hesitated a moment, as if considering the matter. "All right," he replied. "Can't say no to a good chicken stew."

Natty led the way, shuffling ahead with a surprisingly rapid gait. Sadie trotted to catch up with him.

Natty said very little on the walk over, emitting only a series of grunts as they shambled down the sidewalk. After a few brief attempts at conversation, Sadie fell silent too. Natty was a man on a mission for chicken stew.

Los Pollitos was relatively quiet for a weeknight, with a few patrons scattered here and there. Inside, the warm air smelled of cumin and garlic. Sadie breathed in appreciatively.

Elena Garza, who must have been home from college for an extended weekend stay, raised her eyebrows at Sadie as she glanced at Natty. Then she ushered them both to a table toward the back.

After they settled in and placed their orders, Sadie offered Natty the basket of tortilla chips.

"Can't eat them. They gum up my bridgework." Natty removed his fedora and set it on the chair beside him. He ran his gnarled hand over his gray crew cut. "Say now, this ain't a date, is it? I don't want to get crossways with Edwin Marshall. I could've whipped him in my younger days, but I'm not so sure about now."

The tortilla chip Sadie had been chewing caught in her throat, and she coughed, her eyes filling with tears. She grabbed her glass of water and downed a gulp, spluttering a little. "Date?" she managed. "No, Mr. Flats, this isn't a date."

"Well, good." Natty sat back, contemplating his coffee. "I remember your daddy. He was a good fellow."

"Thank you. I thought you must have known him." Sadie dabbed at her eyes with her cotton napkin. "I actually asked you to dinner because my granddaughter is writing an essay about the Mountain Crest Railway and Collin Malloy. I was wondering if you would be willing to talk to her about what life was like here in the 1930s."

"Collin Malloy?" Natty folded his arms across his chest, a speculative gleam in his eye. "What does she want to know?"

"Well, we're participating in the treasure hunt for Collin Malloy's pocket watch. I don't know if you've heard about it... We've done some research at the library, and Sara's essay will connect the watch's significance to the way people felt about him and about the town in general during the 1930s. I thought perhaps you might remember something about Malloy or the watch."

Elena brought over a tray weighted with enchiladas for Sadie and a brimming bowl of chicken tortilla soup for Natty. After she placed the plates on the table, Natty surprised Sadie by bowing his head for and offering a familiar dinner blessing. Sadie quickly closed her eyes, and then echoed his amen when he finished.

Natty grabbed his soup spoon and ate quickly. Though his hands trembled, and though the soup was a trifle thin, he made quick work of it without splattering any on his cravat. Sadie watched for a moment as the dignified elderly man ate until she remembered the reason she had invited him to dinner.

"Natty, do you remember when Silver Peak took up a collection for the pocket watch? It must have been a big deal." She took a bite of her enchiladas and sat back.

"All of Silver Peak loved Collin Malloy." Natty swirled the remnants of the broth around with his spoon. "He was a star, you know. He went on to Hollywood and became a star in the movie musicals."

"Yes, sir. It was quite an accomplishment. That's why the town banded together to give him the watch." Sadie took another bite of her enchiladas.

"What do you know about the watch?" Natty dropped his spoon with a clatter.

"Not much." It was true, and somehow, she didn't feel the time was right to tell him about finding it on the train. "It must have been quite a treasure."

"Yep, it was." Natty took a deep breath, closing his eyes. "I remember like it was yesterday. It was a lot heavier than I expected, and it sparkled so pretty in the sun."

Sadie set her fork aside. Had she heard him right? "Wait. Did you—did you actually see the watch?"

"See it?" Natty's eyes snapped open and he pounded the table with his fist, causing the water to splash around in their glasses. "I held it in my hands. I was only nine years old, but I was the most trusted delivery boy in Silver Peak. Folks liked to hire me because I was so fast. I ran near 'bout everywhere I went. Didn't slow down till I went into the infantry in 1941."

Sadie's heart leaped in her chest. "You held it in your hands?"

"Yes, I did. I remember opening the box and seeing all those diamonds catch the light. It was worth a lot of money too. Everyone in the town had contributed. I even gave a penny to the fund. It was all I could spare from my delivery money." A shadow fell across Natty's face. "I had to give up going to school. My pa had TB. My family needed me to work. Even just one of those diamonds would have turned our lives around."

Sadie held still. Years of teaching high school students had taught her that people often said more when she just let them talk, rather than peppering them and leading them with questions.

Whatever fountain had opened within Natty dried up, though. He fell silent, his eyes dimming as he remembered the past.

"I imagine so," she said, breaking the lengthy pause.

"What?" Natty gazed at her, his eyebrows drawn together.

"I imagine those diamonds were valuable." She took another bite of her dinner and chewed quietly, hoping that Natty would say something more. But the old man seemed to be done talking. He sat in silence as she ate, his mind seemingly fixed on something distant. As she finished her dinner, Natty sipped on his coffee. Sadie cleared her throat. "Mr. Flats, I have to wonder whatever happened to that watch. The entire town contributed to a fund so that they could give something beautiful and worthy to their favorite adopted son. But from what we can tell by looking back at records and articles, Malloy never received the watch. What became of it? You say you saw it, and even held it in your hands."

"What are you saying?" Natty glared at her. "Are you saying that I took it?"

"No, no, not at all." Heat flooded Sadie's cheeks and she blinked rapidly. "I just wondered—" She wished now that she would have asked Edwin to meet them at the restaurant. His solid, unruffled demeanor might have kept the conversation from going in this direction.

"If I had stolen that watch, which I didn't, we would have been rich. My Pa wouldn't have died the year after." Natty's voice rose, and he fixed her with a baleful glare. "We could have sent him to the sanitarium."

"Please, Mr. Flats," Sadie glanced around as people began to notice them. "That's not what I meant at all."

"I would have thought that your pa raised you better than to go around accusing good, decent folks of theft. That watch was entrusted to me when I was nine years old. If the people in this town didn't trust me, they wouldn't have asked me to carry it to the opera house." He banged one fist on the table again and stood.

"I am so sorry, Mr. Flats," she entreated in a hushed tone. "I didn't mean to offend you, and I wasn't implying that you had taken the watch. I just wondered what happened when Collin Malloy left town—"

Natty grabbed his hat and set it firmly on his head. "I take my leave of you, Mrs. Speers." Then he hobbled out, leaving her at the table.

The few patrons who had been watching this tableau with interest turned back to their dinners, and Sadie was left blessedly alone. As Elena walked by with an order for another table, Sadie asked for the check.

Why had Natty been so defensive? Sadie drained the dregs of her coffee cup and then gathered her things to go. Had she really struck that much of a nerve? He did admit that he had held the watch in his hand. How, then, did it get from Natty to seat 13C?

As she turned to leave, she nearly collided with Pastor Don Sweeting and his wife. "Oh, sorry about that, you two. It's been quite a day."

"No worries," Pastor Don said with a chuckle. "I know what you mean. I officiated at a wedding today and I am just about beat. Jeanne promised me dinner out as my reward."

"Oh, that's right! You officiated at Darcy Burke's wedding." Sadie tugged on her jacket. "How was it?"

"The ceremony was beautiful." Jeanne whipped her cell phone out of her leather purse. "I took pictures, because the decorations were divine. Totally vintage. You would have loved it. Do you want to see?" She swiped her finger over the screen and handed it to Sadie. "Her dress was antique—I think it was from the 1920s."

Sadie scrolled slowly through the pictures, exclaiming along with Jeanne. Darcy made an adorable bride, her dark hair bundled to look like it had been bobbed, and a cute little mob cap veil tilted cheekily over her eye. The groom and his attendants looked like they had stepped out of a Fred Astaire movie, and her bridesmaids wore lavender copies of her bridal gown.

"Lovely!" She smiled at Jeanne. "Thanks for sharing your pictures."

"Wait, there's a few more." Jeanne flicked the screen forward with a graceful finger. "Just look at her cake. Isn't it pretty?"

Sadie nodded, but it was the other objects on the cake table that held her interest. She peered intently at the phone. "Is there any way to make the picture bigger?"

"Sure." Jeanne magnified the screen.

Sadie's missing Fire-King mugs and hot chocolate set sat on Darcy's cake table. A sinking feeling settled into the pit of her stomach. At least this explained where they'd gone and why Darcy had fled once she spied Sadie in the parking lot. But it seemed odd that Jack wouldn't have noticed them.

"Where is Darcy now?" She handed the phone back to Jeanne. "I suppose she's on her honeymoon."

"No." Pastor Don shook his head. "It sounded like they were low on money, so I think that she and her husband are back at work. I waived my usual fee because I wanted to give them a head start."

Sadie gave the Sweetings a big hug. "Jeanne, feed this man some Mexican food," she ordered with a chuckle. "He's earned that, at least."

The Sweetings drifted over to their table, and Sadie paid the bill up front. As she walked out into the clear, cold, night, a million stars twinkled up in the vast dark sky. She exhaled, her breath making a little cloud of mist. Now she knew that Darcy had taken some of her antiques, did it follow that she would steal other things?

Darcy was Jack's niece, so maybe she had heard some of those stories about her great-grandfather, John Fitzgerald. Did any of the Fitzgerald family legends include the day gangsters came to Silver Peak in search of Collin Malloy? Could Darcy have known—or at least suspected—that the watch was hidden on the train?

Would a woman who couldn't afford a honeymoon steal a diamond pocket watch?

15

As Sadie drove east from downtown Silver Peak, she glanced in her rearview mirror. The town's namesake mountain loomed large in the reflection, and Sadie was again struck by how beautiful the region was. Even though she had been born in Silver Peak and lived nearly all of her life there, she never tired of the breathtaking vistas that surrounded her hometown. Today the sun glinted off a layer of pristine new snow at the very peak of the mountain, contrasting against the deep green pine forests and clear blue sky.

She reluctantly pulled her gaze back to the road as it took her again to the edge of town. She was on a mission. The night before, on the way home from Los Pollitos, Sadie had determined that she still needed to figure out what Natty Flats might know about the watch. But how to do that without offending him further?

That was why, after the morning routine at the Antique Mine, with Julie enduring the racket from Fleagle's roofing crew, she found herself once more driving out to see Joe Martinez. She slowed the Tahoe and pulled into the mostly empty parking lot of the Plaza and parked in front of Joe's Pawn Shop, where Joe was setting up a display of skis and ski equipment.

"Good morning." Sadie waved to Joe Martinez as she approached the store. "Do you have a minute or two?"

"Sure, Sadie. Come on in. You're becoming a regular!" Joe's dark eyes twinkled. He held the door open for Sadie as she made her way into the shop. "Did you ever find the owner of that earring?"

Sadie stifled a laugh. "The owner came back to claim it the next day."

"I'm glad to hear it." Joe handed her the coffee. "So how can I help you, Sadie?"

As Joe puttered around, dragging a chair up to his desk and pouring coffee into Styrofoam cups for the two of them, Sadie took a mental inventory of all she meant to say.

"The day I brought you the earring, Natty Flats also came in. Do you mind if I ask what he sold you? I love antiques, and someone like Natty might offer items that are truly unique." She sipped her coffee, savoring it as she waited.

"Unique?" Joe laughed. "I suppose you could call it that. I've been in this business for years, and I always seem to get the same items—electronics, jewelry, musical instruments. This was the first time anyone tried to sell me coconuts."

"Coconuts?" Sadie spluttered into her coffee. "What do you mean?"

Joe gestured to a rack behind her. "Coconuts. Carved coconuts, and a bunch of other small stuff that doesn't really amount to much. Natty told me they were all he had. Well, what could I do? I bought it all."

Sadie set down her coffee cup and rose. "Do you mind if I take a look?"

Joe shook his head, his mouth twisted in a rueful grin. "Go right ahead. I doubt you'll find much of interest, though."

Sadie bent down to peer at the shelf Joe had indicated. Sure enough, a line of carved coconuts teetered precariously on the shelf. A hodgepodge of other items, dusty and faintly smelling of smoke, were shoved onto the shelf beside them.

"This is what he sold you? When I saw him, he didn't have any of this with him."

"No, first he brought an old watch." Sadie felt a kick of adrenaline as Joe walked over to the jewelry case and unlocked it, but it quickly subsided when she saw what he was taking from the case. "It's just a battered old thing—a Timex. I bought it, and Natty told me he had more stuff to show me. He brought it all in to me later that afternoon, pulling it in a little red wagon like you see kids with."

Sadie took the watch and flipped it over in her palm. Joe was right. It was a Timex from the 1940s, the kind that took a licking and kept on ticking. Sadie guessed the watch might have been issued to Natty when he enlisted. Judging by the scratched case, cracked crystal, and worn band, this one had indeed taken quite a licking over the years. Sadie wound the stem, put it to her ear, and smiled as she was rewarded by a faint ticking sound.

"In all honesty, the wagon was probably worth more than everything else he brought in it. I offered to buy it, because it was a nice Radio Flyer"—Joe shrugged—"but he didn't want to part with it." He took the watch from Sadie and put it back into the case.

Sadie shook her head. Edwin was right. Natty's finances were in pretty bad shape. These few items, judging by their age, were remnants of his youth. In addition to the carved coconuts, Natty had brought in an assortment of sorry-looking small baskets, two small satin pillows with palm trees and the names of South Pacific islands embroidered on them, and a variety of other small cheap items that were likely souvenirs obtained during his infantry service.

"Like I said, I usually don't buy junk like this, but I felt bad for him," Joe said.

A small black book with a thick paper cover caught Sadie's eye. The jaunty script typeface read "Photographs & Memories" in silver ink against the textured paper. "Could I see that?" she asked.

He slid it toward her. Sadie opened it and saw a series of old square black-and-white photos with scalloped edges, also apparently from Natty's time in the service—perhaps from basic training, as they appeared to be at an unidentified base, rather than on the battlefield. It was one of the old photo albums that were made up from the photos themselves, bound into a book, rather than being mounted to a page.

She was easily able to pick out Natty from among the other soldiers in the pictures, and it fascinated her to see him as a much younger man, standing tall and proud in his neat uniform, looking happy among his buddies. Old photos could have value—in her shop, she sometimes sold collections of old family photos that she'd found at estate sales—but their real value was in the memories they held.

While her practical side—the side of a child raised by Depression-era parents—understood his decision to sell these items, another part of her couldn't bear for Natty to be deprived of his story. Everything she did related to the stories people had to tell.

Her store was filled with treasures that others left behind, precious objects that conveyed a tale from one generation to another. No one should have to give up their story for a bag or two of groceries.

"Joe, I want everything that Natty sold to you," she said. "Name your price."

"Are you serious?" His brown eyes glinted in surprise. "None of this stuff is worth anything. You'll never be able to sell any of it."

Sadie shook her head. "I'm not planning to sell it. Just name your price."

A plan was forming in the back of her mind. Everyone needed to tell their story. Every person needed to feel valued. Most importantly, everyone needed to eat.

She started bringing the items over to the counter, stacking them as high as they would go without tipping over.

"Ten bucks, maybe? I dunno." Joe stuffed the pillow into a large trash bag. "To be honest, I feel bad making you pay anything."

Sadie laughed. "Don't be ridiculous, Joe. You're running a business here. How much did you pay for them? It wouldn't be fair to give you a penny less."

Joe gave her a sheepish look. "Two hundred dollars?" He reached below the counter and pulled out a carbon receipt book and showed her the receipt made out to Natty for that amount.

Sadie smiled, touched by his generosity. "Okay, then. Not a dollar less." She rooted around in her purse for her wallet and pulled out some cash, then handed it to him. "You're a good man, Joe." She went back for the coconuts, adding them to the bag.

Joe retrieved the watch from the jewelry case. "This too?"

Sadie nodded. "Absolutely. I'll put that in my purse."

Joe handed over the watch, then stepped back and peered at her as if her senses might momentarily have left her. "Anything else I can get for you today, Sadie?"

"No, I think I have everything I need." She grabbed the trash bag with the coconuts and other items. It was bulky but light.

"Wait, you want me to deliver that so you don't have to carry it around?" Joe asked. He chuckled, but Sadie knew his offer was sincere.

"Thank you, Joe, but I'm parked right outside." Sadie turned to go, but as she did so she realized the fancy guitar she'd seen when she visited a few days ago was gone. "Looks like you sold the guitar and amp you had, Joe. Congratulations!"

"I'll say." Joe came around to hold the door open for her. "Someone came by and picked it up yesterday. And good for him. That guitar is known as the Holy Grail among serious players, and the amp is pretty coveted for its tone. I was thinking of listing them both for an auction online, because I figured I could get a bidding war going."

"Is it really worth that much?" While musical instruments were not her specialty, she knew that guitars could fetch quite a hefty price if they were antique or rare…but could something found in a pawn shop be that valuable?

"Oh yeah. I had it marked at seven thousand dollars, thinking some wealthy tourist might wander in and find it this week. Wishful thinking, I guess. But then this guy came in and plunked down the full amount in cash. Could've knocked me over with a feather."

"Wow. Well, that should make up for a few slow days." She hoisted the bag onto one shoulder. "Joe, thanks so much. You've helped me more than you know."

Joe shrugged, shaking his head. "I don't think I did much other than rob you of two hundred dollars."

Sadie smiled as she headed out the door with Natty's treasures, but as she trekked back to her Tahoe, her mind raced. These items might be exactly what she needed to get Natty to talk to her again.

The way she had originally approached Natty was all wrong. He was old, he was tired, and he needed money. When she began questioning him, he grew angry out of pride—just as Edwin had suspected he might. Now it was up to her not only to repair the damage, but if possible, and if Natty was willing, help Natty tell his story to Sara. His input would be so valuable for Sara's essay, and his experience as one of the oldest residents of Silver Peak was something she wanted her granddaughter to become acquainted with. But more than that, she felt that sharing his story would be good for Natty and would help others appreciate him and his place in Silver Peak's history.

She opened the door to the Antique Mine to find Julie at the counter, helping Robert Smith look through the box of film star stills.

Julie looked up from the photographs. "Hi, Sadie. Goodness, what have you got there?"

"Here." Robert made a sudden, swift movement, taking the bag from her shoulder and lowering it to the floor. "Let me get that for you."

Again, there was that charm. Mr. Smith was graceful, fluid, and endearing despite all her efforts to remain wary. "Thanks, Robert."

"I'm really glad you're here, Sadie," Julie said. "Robert was asking about one of the pictures you have hanging in the display. He wondered how much you'd like for it."

"Oh!" Sadie looked at her display. "Well, I'd rather not sell any of them right now, but maybe after the festival is over. Will you still be around then?"

"I'm not sure." He walked over to the display and studied it. "Are you sure I can't buy one of them off you today?"

"I'm sorry." Sadie gave him a regretful smile. "That display is more for informational and historic purposes right now than to show off the photos as merchandise. There are many interesting stills in that basket, though. Feel free to comb through them all. I'll cut you a deal if you buy more than two."

Julie suddenly gasped. "Oh! Sadie, doesn't he look just like Collin Malloy?"

Sadie smiled to herself. It was good to hear someone else confirm what she'd seen in Robert.

Robert looked surprised and focused on the large portrait of Malloy in the center of the display. "Really?"

"Oh yes!" Julie breathed. "You look exactly like him."

Sadie smiled at him. "Maybe you're related!"

Robert laughed and shook his head. "Nah, my dad grew up in an orphanage. 'John Smith' is the kind of name you get when no one knows who your parents were."

Julie looked disappointed. "Oh, that's too bad. How exciting would that have been? To have a relative of Collin Malloy right here in Silver Peak?"

"That's way too romantic for a humble musician like me." Robert tapped the counter with his fingertips, then turned to Sadie. "I'm headed to Denver for a few days. Maybe when I get back, I'll see if I can talk you out of that photograph."

"Are you that tired of the racket from the roofers?" Sadie teased.

Robert laughed. "Nah. Job interviews." He flashed them both a smile. "See you later, ladies. Wish me luck!"

He strolled out of the shop with his jacket carelessly thrown over one shoulder—a picture of masterful nonchalance.

"Speaking of racket, that mess over at Spike's is making my head pound." Julie shuffled the movie stills back into the basket, fanning them out with an elegant gesture. "How long do you think it will take them?"

"I'm not sure. Maybe a week, probably more."

Sadie picked up the garbage bag full of Natty's trinkets. She was certain Natty had the answers to all the riddles concerning Collin Malloy. Once she answered those questions, she could press forward with finding out what had happened to her mystery man and the pocket watch.

"What have you got there?" Julie looked at the bag. "You looked like Santa when you came in, with it slung over your shoulder."

Sadie chuckled. "I don't know whether I should be flattered or put out. Don't worry; this isn't stuff for the shop. I'll be done with it by the end of the day."

"Okay."

As Sadie turned to go back to the storage room, a luxurious, chocolate-colored fur coat hanging from a coat tree caught her eye. "Where did that come from?"

Julie held out the fur, stroking it with her palm. "Mrs. Elliott left it behind. Can you believe she'd forget something like this? She and Mr. Elliott came in with Robert, but they left just a few minutes before you arrived."

"The Elliotts? I hope they were friendlier this time." Sadie pretended to focus on the fur, but her mind was preoccupied with Julie's answer.

"As friendly as the Elliotts ever are, I suppose. They ran me ragged again. I had no time to help Robert until they were gone. You know, Robert's come in before. He was the guy who wanted to look through the movie stills the other day. Anyway, as soon as the Elliotts left, I saw that she'd left the fur behind. Robert ran out with it, trying to flag them down in the street, but they couldn't hear him. The roofers were making too much noise." Julie yawned and stretched. "Is it five o'clock yet? I'm worn out already."

"Did the Elliotts buy anything?"

"More costume pieces. Nothing as valuable as you sold them the other day." Julie pointed to the empty spots in the jewelry case. "She said she wanted one last big haul before they returned to Denver, which I gathered is in the next day or so."

Julie reached for the coat. "Do you want me to send it down to the police station? Or should we call around until we find them?"

"I know exactly where they're staying."

Sadie grabbed the coat. It was so soft she had trouble grasping it, because the fur kept sliding out of her hands. Even so, there was something odd about it. She rubbed the fur between her fingers. She was certain that, like the earring, and perhaps like the Elliotts themselves, the coat was masquerading as something it wasn't.

Sara bounded into the shop, typing on her phone as she walked. "Hey, Grandma!"

"Walking and texting at the same time?" Sadie laughed and shook her head. "I like to think of myself as coordinated, but I'd end up looking like a pretzel on the floor."

Sara laughed. "I want to finish my essay before I go to Dad's house this weekend. Will you take me to meet this Natty Flats guy? I bet he can really help me out."

"Yes." A sudden intuition flashed through Sadie. She knew exactly how to win Natty over. "Let's stop by Arbuckle's on our way out."

"Okay." Sara continued tapping away on her phone screen.

"Julie, I'll take this coat over to the B and B this afternoon. Sara and I will be gone for a couple of hours, but I'll be back before five."

Sadie handed the fur coat to her granddaughter and grabbed the bag of Natty's possessions as they headed for her car. With any luck, by the time the sun went down, Sara would have the information she needed for her essay, and Sadie would know for sure if the Elliotts were involved in taking the watch.

16

Sadie carefully navigated the Tahoe, her eyes fixed firmly on the twisting, narrow mountain road. The two coffee cups in the front cup holders sloshed precariously, and she slowed the SUV, easing her foot off the accelerator. Sadie was an experienced mountain driver, but the meandering road and pitted gravel surface made driving a challenge, compounded by her unfamiliarity with the area. Even in her hikes with Hank or her rides on her horse, Scout, she'd never ventured this far. Natty had definitely chosen a secluded place as his retreat.

Following the commands of her GPS, she veered off the main road and bounced slowly up a rocky, winding path. A cluster of pine trees gave way to an astonishing vista, and Sadie stopped the Tahoe, inhaling sharply as she drank in the view. From this vantage point, Silver Peak was tucked into a purple hollow at the foot of the mountain, sheltered and snug. Golden aspens glowed against the deep green pine backdrop around Silver Peak. She could pick out the opera house, the library, the high school, and other landmarks on Main Street, which intersected Silver Peak like a bookmark in an old favorite hardcover. Rolling foothills undulated around her hometown, rising and falling gently like waves upon the sea.

No wonder Natty liked it up here. Imagine, waking every morning to a view like this—a perfect landscape reflecting God's majesty.

"Wow," Sara breathed.

"Yes." Sadie knew that mere words could never express how beautiful this view was.

She gazed out a little while longer, pausing to clarify her purpose in this trip. Everyone needed to feel valued, and everyone deserved a chance to tell their story.

They would just ask Natty to tell the story.

Sadie said a quick silent prayer for strength and guidance, and then shifted the Tahoe back into drive. She continued down the curving dirt road until she came upon a ramshackle cabin off in a clearing. Judging by its architectural lines, the cabin had originally been a two-room affair, constructed of tightly hewn logs. Over time, however, the owners had expanded it, adding rooms off to either side using two-by-fours that had been painted. The coats of paint had faded and peeled over time, giving the structure a disheveled, unkempt look.

She eased the Tahoe to a halt beside the rickety fence confining Natty's property and got out. Sara joined her, banging the passenger side door shut. As they began walking toward the cabin, Sadie could feel the lack of oxygen. She was used to Silver Peak's elevation, but this was considerably higher, and she slowed her pace to adjust for the thin air.

A herd of mongrel dogs, in every color and size, thundered to the front gate, barking and yapping in an effusive canine chorus.

"How cute!" Sara strode over to the fence, apparently not feeling the oxygen deficit as much as her grandmother. "I want to take them all home with me."

Natty stepped out onto the front porch, splendidly arrayed in a faded blue silk cravat, clean white cotton shirt, and gray wool pants. He cradled a shotgun in the crook of his arm. "What can I do for you, Mrs. Speers?" He eyed them warily and did not call off his dogs. Once he caught a glimpse of Sara, though, he set his shotgun aside.

"Mr. Flats, this is my granddaughter, Sara. I spoke with you about her the other night. We brought you some coffee." She held the paper cups from Arbuckle's aloft. "I guess you could say we're bribing you in exchange for your memories of Silver Peak."

"Coffee?" Natty squinted at the cups. "I hope it ain't that fancy kind with all the whipped cream and sugar syrup. That stuff turns my stomach. If I want a dessert, I'll eat a slice of pie, not drink a dolled-up coffee."

"The coffee's black. I'm like you—I like to taste my coffee, not the cream. But we brought pie too." She nodded toward Sara, who lifted the plastic bag in her hand so Natty could see it. "Apple cranberry."

Sara watched them both silently. One of the dogs stuck his muzzle through the fence and licked her hand. She held back a little, perhaps as daunted by Natty as Roz and Sadie had been at her age.

Natty nodded, his shoulders slumping a little. "All right, then." He turned to the canine chorus. "Dogs, go home."

The pack of yelping mutts pricked up their ears and scattered, tails wagging.

Sadie picked her way over to the gate and held out the coffee. "You've got a mighty pretty view here, Mr. Flats. I must say I envy you."

Natty ambled down the front steps. "It sure is. I never tire of seeing it. When I was overseas, I thought about the view from my mountain every morning." He accepted the cup of coffee with a grateful nod. "Seeing as how you brought dessert, I suppose you two can come in."

Sadie gave a respectful nod. "Thank you, sir."

Natty turned and shuffled up the steps. Sadie let Sara pass through the gate, which gave a mournful squeak as she opened it. A few of the dogs pricked up their ears as they walked past, but none of them uttered a sound.

Natty's gun still rested against the wall of the porch. Sadie suppressed a grin. At least he hadn't taken it inside. Perhaps that was a good sign.

She ducked into Natty's cabin, and cozy warmth enveloped her. A few oil lanterns sputtered brightly, dotting the room with light. A heavy oaken table sat squarely between two plaid sofas, and a worn leather chair sat next to the fire. A lithograph of the Virgin Mary graced the mantel. Sadie leaned forward and examined it closely. It had to be from the early 1920s, judging by the condition of the paper and the faded colors.

The overall effect of the cabin was clean and snug—not at all the kind of environment she would have expected an eccentric mountain recluse to live in.

Natty waved them toward one of the plaid couches. "Have a seat."

Sara hung back a little, waiting for Sadie to take the lead. Sadie beckoned her over to the couch and they sat. They took the pie slices out of the bag.

"Here you go. They packed plastic forks too. Arbuckle's gets their pies from Maggie Price at the Market, and her pie is wonderful. I hope you enjoy it."

Natty sat opposite her and took the Styrofoam container. "Not too many folks appreciate a good pie. It's all in the crust," he said after a few bites. "This one here is good, but not as good as my ma used to make."

"I understand that," Sadie replied. The pie was tasty, but nothing beat the piecrust that her mother used to roll out on a floured wooden board. Sara quietly ate her pie, glancing around the cabin and at their host.

They ate in silence for a few moments, and Sadie waited to see if the pie would put Natty in a more talkative mood. Even if it wasn't homemade, the pie was making her pretty happy. She hoped it would have the same effect on Natty.

Everything about the little cabin told a story, she mused as she glanced around. The starched cotton curtains at the window had edges trimmed in crocheted lace—the delicate details that used to be the fundamental mark of good housekeeping. Though the plaid sofas were faded and worn, they were clean and still had some spring left in the cushions. There was a faint odor of tobacco smoke but no ashtrays, which meant Natty smoked outside.

This was the home of a man who had nothing to prove. This was the type of home that pointed to old-fashioned values of honesty, cleanliness, and thrift. It was in direct contrast to Natty's showy attire, which, though worn, still garnered attention.

"Mr. Flats," she began hesitantly, "my granddaughter would love to hear about Collin Malloy and the diamond pocket watch." She glanced over at Sara, giving her an encouraging look.

"Yes, sir." Sara was shy in front of this elderly man, but she spoke clearly and firmly. "I brought my phone. I thought I could record our conversation."

Natty grunted, sucking his teeth a little, and slanted a glance at Sadie. "You going to accuse me of stealing that watch again?"

Sara looked at Sadie, who quickly said, "We don't think you had anything to do with the watch going missing, Mr. Flats. I didn't mean to imply that at all. I'm so sorry for the misunderstanding."

Natty nodded, studying Sadie with narrow eyes. Then he turned to Sara and said, "Well?"

Sara took a deep breath and pressed the record button on her phone. "Could you tell me what it was like, being a delivery boy back in the 1930s? Was it exciting to be entrusted with something as valuable as Collin Malloy's pocket watch?"

"Exciting? Ha! It could be downright dangerous." Natty leaned forward, a glimmer showing in the depths of his faded blue eyes. "I almost got shot up by gangsters!"

Sadie tilted her head to one side. Had she heard right? "Gangsters?" Sara gasped.

"Yes, missy. You wouldn't think gangsters would care about Silver Peak, but they did. At least, they cared about it because Collin Malloy was here, and he owed them lots of money. He was what we called a high roller, and he got into big trouble. Mr. Fitzgerald, the train engineer, came to find me that spring morning. He had just brought those gangsters into town on the train, and they were going to get the money from Malloy, by hook or by crook."

Natty paused, took a sip of his coffee, and grimaced. "Sure is strong. I like my own coffee better."

Sadie nodded. If she said anything, she might derail his train of thought, and he was traveling right down the path that interested her most. Judging by her wide eyes, Sara was enthralled too.

"So that day I was on my way to the opera house with the watch, and I decided I wanted to see it. So I opened the box right there in the street. My, my, it was pretty. Sparkled like all the stars in the sky. Then Mr. Fitzgerald ran toward me. He was sweating, and his face was all red and blotchy. He told me to hide the watch in Engine No. 2, because the gangsters were after Collin Malloy, and then get out of town and lay low for a few days afterward. So I did what he told me.

"I saw them gangsters as I was running to the rail yard. They come squealing up Main Street in a big fancy car, and I knew Mr. Fitzgerald was right. They were after Malloy and might steal the watch in payment for his debts. So I hid the watch box under Mr. Fitzgerald's seat in the engine where it couldn't be seen.

"After that, I went and stayed under a bridge outside of town for a few days, like Mr. Fitzgerald told me." He looked up at them, the light from one of the oil lamps bathing his wrinkled face in a warm glow.

"You stayed by yourself? Under a bridge?" Sara was incredulous. "How old were you?"

"I was nine."

A million questions swirled through Sadie's mind, so she picked the one that floated to the top first. "Did Mr. Fitzgerald save Collin Malloy from the gangsters too?"

"Yes, he did. I heard tell he spirited him out of town with the parcels and luggage." Natty gave a dry, wheezing laugh and slapped his knee. "Can you beat it? What a way to land in Hollywood! The gangsters never thought to look there, so Malloy was safe."

Sara giggled. "That's pretty cool."

Sadie grabbed her purse and withdrew her journal. She flipped to the page where she'd jotted down the message from John Fitzgerald's log. "We saw this in the engineer's logbook at the public library," she explained, holding the book out to him. "We're guessing the asterisk, the star, was Collin Malloy?"

"Yeah, probably so." Natty squinted at the paper. "I can't see your writing so good, but that sounds about right."

"It says, 'Moved star west. 13C. Time will tell.' Does 13C mean anything to you?"

Natty shrugged. "Sure. 13C was Malloy's favorite seat."

17

Sadie stared at Natty Flats while several pieces of the puzzle clicked into place.

"I remember that he always bought the same seat on the trips in and out of town for good luck. He was superstitious and afraid if he sat in another seat, he'd sing badly." Natty looked toward Sara, eyeing her phone. "I liked Mr. Fitzgerald, and he liked me, so he let me hang around the rail yard. I learned a lot just by watching him work."

If 13C was Malloy's favorite seat, then it could explain how the watch ended up where she was sitting. In all likilihood, Mr. Fitzgerald moved the watch from under his seat in the engine, planting it in the seat that Collin Malloy preferred. Apparently Malloy had never come back to get it. Sadie tucked the scrap of paper back in her purse.

"I wonder what happened to the watch after that," Sara wondered out loud, echoing Sadie's thoughts.

"I dunno." Natty shrugged. "When I asked Mr. Fitzgerald what he was going to do with it, he told me to hush, that he'd take care of it. That's all I know. Never saw him again." Natty sagged against the couch. "Is that any help to you, missy?"

"Yes, it's great," Sara said. "Now we know a lot more about the day the watch went missing. Maybe it will help us find the watch again."

Natty nodded slowly. "That'd be nice. I'd love to see it again."

Sadie had an idea. "I have a proposal for you, Mr. Flats. I know you must have a ton of stories about Silver Peak. Would you consider coming to my antique store sometime to give a talk? You can tell us what it was like back then."

"Well—I don't know." Natty ruffled his hand through his hair. "I don't much like going into town, unless I need to. My clothes ain't so fine as they used to be. I used to have some fine tailored suits. They've faded now, though."

"You look fine, Mr. Flats. Most importantly, you have a wealth of knowledge about our town's past." She gave him her most beseeching look, the one she would turn on for the most stubborn of antique dealers. "I'll pay you one hundred dollars. What do you say?"

Natty blinked rapidly, then stuck out his hand. "All right then. You have yourself a deal."

Sadie's heart glowed as she reached out to shake his hand. "There's one more thing. As both an apology for our misunderstanding the other night, and from one storyteller to another, I brought your things back from Joe's Pawn Shop. I know each souvenir has a story."

Tears misted suddenly in Natty's eyes and his Adam's apple bobbed up and down above his faded cravat. "Thank you, Mrs. Speers. That's very kind of you."

"Will you see us to the car? We'll get your things out, and then we should be getting back to town." She stood, offering him her arm.

As Sadie walked out of the ramshackle cabin on Natty's arm, with Sara trailing behind them, she felt ridiculous for ever having been afraid of Natty. Judging others by their appearances was a terrible way to live life. Was anything or anyone as they really seemed? As she retrieved Natty's tattered belongings, she flicked a glance at Mrs. Elliott's faux fur.

"Mrs. Speers, Miz Sara, I surely did enjoy your company today." Natty helped Sara into the SUV and closed the door. "If I can help you track down that watch, just let me know."

"Mr. Flats, you are definitely our partner in crime," Sadie told him with a laugh. Sara thanked him again for his help and then clambered into the Tahoe.

As Sadie drove away with Sara, she felt a glow of satisfaction when she glanced back in her rearview mirror. Natty stood with the bag next to him, looking through the photos in the small album she'd recovered for him from Joe's Pawn Shop.

"I'm going to write my essay right now," Sara remarked as they pulled up into Alice's driveway. "I want to finish the essay and turn it in before I go to Dad's house this weekend."

Sadie smiled at her granddaughter's rare show of unbridled enthusiasm. Sara didn't normally get excited over books or writing. She was much more of an animal lover and outdoorsy type, though she also spent a great deal of time texting her friends. So it was especially nice to see her so thrilled about writing a good old-fashioned essay.

As soon as Sadie stopped the car, Sara hopped out of the Tahoe and gave her a quick hug. She gave Sadie a self-conscious smile that flashed her braces. "Thanks, Grandma! Talk to you later."

Sara waved and headed inside.

Sadie put the car in reverse and backed down the driveway. She only had one errand left before she could relieve Julie at the Antique Mine and close up for the day. She needed to return Grace Elliott's coat to her. It was time to satisfy her curiosity about the Elliotts once and for all.

She slowed the Tahoe to a stop outside the white two-story Victorian home that Jane and Jerry Remington had renovated into an inn. A quaint wooden sign proclaimed, in elegant script, "Silver Peak Bed-and-Breakfast." Jane had surrounded the porch with fall colors—deep purple mums and tawny marigolds made a lovely contrast to the white wooden porch steps.

She took the steps two at a time, adjusting the fur coat so it hung gracefully over her arm. Sadie opened the B and B's front door to a rising tide of voices.

"Look, we didn't stay an extra night. We shouldn't be charged for it." Thomas Elliott's voice grew louder with each syllable. "This is outrageous."

"Our check-out policy clearly states that if you stay past noon, you will be charged for an extra day. I was very clear about that when you checked in." Jane, normally so composed, looked strained and close to tears. "Since it's four thirty right now, we have to charge you for another day."

"I didn't know until an hour ago that I would be called to Denver this evening," Thomas Elliott thundered. "You're taking advantage of an emergency to cheat us out of another night's stay."

Sadie cleared her throat, shutting the door firmly behind her.

Jane jumped at the sound. "Oh, hi, Sadie," she said. "I'll be with you in just a moment."

"Actually, I just need to see Mrs. Elliott." She held out the fur. "She left this in my shop."

"Grace!" Thomas hollered, so loudly that Jane and Sadie both winced. "Get down here!"

A clatter of footsteps sounded on the wooden stairs, and Grace Elliott breezed into the vestibule. "Oh, good." She grabbed the fur off of Sadie's arm. "I'm so glad I don't have to trek back over to your store to retrieve it."

"You're welcome," Sadie replied, although Grace hadn't thanked her. "Can I speak to you for a moment?"

Grace tugged on her coat. "I suppose so. Thomas, quit being cranky. Pay the stupid bill so we can go."

Grace led Sadie to the empty library, closing the door behind them. "What is it? Do you have more interesting jewelry to show me?"

"No, I'm afraid I don't."

Sadie paused. How on earth could she confront Mrs. Elliott with her suspicions that the Elliotts were possibly stealing to cover their debt and make up for their lost income? She didn't want to offend Grace. On the other hand, the Elliotts were the kind of people who went around making demands and then shouting when life didn't go their way—perpetually on the verge of being affronted. So why not dive right in?

"Mrs. Elliott, that fur is a fake, isn't it?"

Grace nodded, folding her arms across her chest. "Yes, it is. I wouldn't be caught dead in real fur."

"And the earring you left in my store—it was a cubic zirconia, but you claimed it was real." There was nothing else to do but put it all out there.

Grace Elliott narrowed her eyes, looking Sadie up and down as coolly as she might appraise a piece of estate jewelry. "So?"

"So why are you passing off fakes as the real thing?" Sadie asked. "Are you using it to defraud someone?"

Grace's face flushed a deep red. "Of course not! How dare you! Thomas knows better than to buy me real diamonds or furs, even for an insurance scam. I loathe real fur and I loathe real diamonds. If you had any idea of the misery the fur and diamond industries cause, you'd understand."

Sadie shook her head. "So your decision to wear fake jewels and fake furs is prompted by environmental activism?"

Grace nodded stiffly. "I know what you must be thinking. My husband owns a billion-dollar corporation, so I should be wearing the real deal. But Thomas started out by creating software that helps make mining more environmentally responsible. What kind of wife would I be if I wore products that perpetuated the very misery we're trying to drive out?"

Sadie had the feeling that the rug was somehow being pulled from beneath her feet. "Then why wear the fakes at all? Doesn't wearing fake fur and diamonds that look real to the average person defeat the purpose of making that kind of stand?"

Grace fidgeted with the collar of her coat and turned her face away from Sadie. "When Thomas's company became successful, suddenly we were going to all these fancy fund-raising dinners and running with a high-class crowd. There's so much pressure to prove your status, to show that you're the equal of everyone else, that I gave in and started buying high-quality fakes that would fool the other couples and make Thomas look good. It's the same with this Japanese firm that's buying us out. They're very concerned with image. The head of this Japanese company absolutely covers his wife with real diamonds, real furs, the whole nine yards." Grace Elliott's voice trailed off and she sighed, her bravado failing her. "We have to look the part to be taken seriously."

A strange feeling of pity tugged at Sadie's heart. Was she really feeling sorry for the imperious and demanding Elliotts? Yes, a little. Grace Elliott was forcing herself to be someone she wasn't so that her husband could be successful—and keep their financial collapse at bay.

But then, looking the part and acting the part were two different things. Sadie felt the Elliotts had gotten a little too good at *acting* the part, but that was none of her business.

"I understand," she replied, and she did. Grace Elliott was human, after all, beneath all her bluster. "I won't say a word. Judging by what I read in the paper, though, it looks like the buyout of your company is a done deal."

Grace rolled her eyes. "It's never over till it's over. I won't believe it until the ink is dry. We're headed back to Denver now, rushing back to sign off on everything without any more delay."

"Well, I will pray for the best." Sadie gave her a reassuring smile. There was one lingering doubt she needed to vanquish before she could finally move on: the Elliotts had been seated behind her on the train.

"And I hope you enjoyed your time in Silver Peak, especially the inaugural train ride. It's a big deal for our town, and I'm so glad we had so many visitors like you and your husband there.

I just hope that when the lights went out for a moment, it didn't spoil the ride for you."

Grace looked genuinely nonplussed. She raised her eyebrows and shook her perfectly coiffed head. "I didn't like it, but it didn't ruin things for me. When the lights went out, we stayed perfectly still." The tiniest hint of a smile reached her eyes for the first time since Sadie had met her. "The shoes I was wearing are hard enough to walk in, without trying to manage it in the dark."

"Grace! Let's go, for crying out loud." Thomas hammered on the closed library door. "Finally got the stupid hotel bill settled. We need to head for Denver immediately."

Grace sighed, cast an apologetic glance at Sadie, and opened the door. "Fine. I'm ready." With a swish of her faux-fur coat, leaving behind a trail of heady, expensive-smelling perfume, Grace Elliott emerged from the library and out of the inn with her husband, leaving a drained-looking Jane behind them.

Sadie wasn't sorry to see them go, she had to admit, but it felt good to cross them off her list as suspects. Though they still *could* have taken the watch, Sadie felt convinced they hadn't. Which left her with her mystery man, wherever he had disappeared to.

"I need chocolate." Jane cradled her head in her hands and closed her eyes. "There are times, especially times like this, when I question my chosen profession."

Sadie patted Jane's back. "You survived!"

"Barely," Jane admitted. She yawned, stretched, and seemed to recover some of her usual good cheer. "Are you headed to the gospel sing-along tonight?"

"I wouldn't miss it for the world. Campfire Chapel and old-timey gospel tunes? What a way to cap off an eventful day. How about you?"

"I was going to go, but I am so drained. I think I'll dive head-first into a bar of chocolate, sink into a bubble bath, and watch mindless TV shows until I fall asleep."

Sadie laughed. "That sounds like a nice, restorative evening. Take care, Jane. I hope you'll recover by Friday, and I'll see you at the dance."

Jane nodded. "That's my hope too."

Sadie checked her reflection once more in the mirror. This denim dress was so comfortable, and the fringed scarf at her neckline made her look pulled together without feeling too dressed up.

A flash of headlights crossed her bedroom wall. That would be Edwin, punctual as always, arriving to take her to Campfire Chapel. She grabbed her purse from the vanity and hurried downstairs.

She paused long enough to pat Hank on her way out the door and flick on the front porch light. Edwin was opening his car door as she rushed down the front steps into the cool autumn evening air.

"Hello, there!" she called. "Been a long time, stranger."

Edwin chuckled. "Sorry. This festival has taken up more of my time than I expected." He kissed her cheek. "You look lovely."

"Thank you." She waited as Edwin opened her door for her and then sank onto the heated leather seat.

She tucked her dress into the side of the seat, and Edwin shut the door. Then he strolled around to his side and got in. "So any progress on figuring out what happened to the watch?"

"Oh, Edwin, so much has happened." She launched into every detail of her day as they drove into town, from her encounter with Natty to returning Mrs. Elliott's fake-fur coat.

"I'm glad Natty was willing to talk to you."

"Oh, me too! Sara and I learned so much from him." Sadie leaned her head back against the seat and smiled. "We found a lot of material at the library, but it really was Natty who filled in all the gaps. We might never have known about John Fitzgerald telling him to hide the watch otherwise. Now we know why Collin Malloy never made it to the opera house that night, and why he never received his watch. We even know how it ended up in my seat."

She went on to tell him what she had learned about Collin Malloy and the watch.

"And then John Fitzgerald died shortly after that?" Edwin asked. He shook his head.

"The night of his last log entry, Jack told me. Of a heart attack. Natty mentioned Fitzgerald was flushed and sweating when he told him to hide the watch. Seems the stress of helping Collin Malloy escape might have been too much for him. And the railway closed down just a few short years after that and the cars went into storage. So apparently that's how the watch managed to stay in the seat all that time."

Edwin briefly turned his head away from the road to smile at her. "Now you just need to figure out where it disappeared to this week."

Sadie sighed. "That's much harder, I'm afraid. I still have no idea who the mystery man was or where he might be."

They fell silent for a moment, and Sadie could see Edwin frowning in the light from the dashboard. She reached over and placed her hand on his arm.

"Sorry, Sadie." He gave her an apologetic smile. "I'm tired. All this running from one event to the next—it's wearing me out."

"It's only two more days. Come Sunday, it will all be over and you will be able to ease up a bit." She squeezed his arm as they pulled into the Campfire Chapel parking lot. "We'll have a huge Sunday dinner together and then relax."

"That sounds great." Edwin pulled into a parking space and shut off the ignition. "Now, let's go hear some good gospel music. I think that will perk us both up."

She smiled, allowing Edwin to help her out of the car. Then, arm in arm, they strolled together into Campfire Chapel. As they walked up the aisle, the Skylarks were already assembling onstage, tuning their instruments.

Spike was there, and as she watched, he flipped open the locks on a guitar case. Then he pulled out a shiny electric guitar, a beautiful instrument completely unlike the beat-up acoustic he usually used on chapel days.

Her heart caught in her throat. Was that the expensive guitar from Joe's Pawn Shop?

18

SADIE BLINKED AND LOOKED AGAIN. THERE WAS NO MISTAKING IT: Spike really was playing a beautiful, expensive-looking guitar. The very one she'd seen at Joe Martinez's shop.

All through the gospel concert, instead of enjoying the music, Sadie argued with herself, trying to justify Spike's purchase of such an expensive instrument. Joe had told her this guitar cost several thousand dollars. Could Spike afford that on top of his roof repairs? Had he purchased the guitar with the intention of selling it in his shop? Perhaps he could recoup his investment or even make enough on the resale to pay for some of his shop's new roof. But if he meant to sell it, would he be playing it here tonight?

She watched, mesmerized, as the guitar flashed under the stage lights, and sighed. Edwin glanced over at her, his eyebrows raised in concern. "Are you all right?"

She nodded. She couldn't very well tell him all her misgivings while they were in the middle of the service. It was a long program too. The music, a mixture of old-time gospel songs in the vein of the Carter Family and country arrangements of old hymns, would have buoyed her up if she hadn't been lost in thoughts about Spike.

As the concert finally drew to a close, Sadie joined in the applause halfheartedly. Edwin looked at her again, giving her a searching, worried glance. She offered him a tiny reassuring smile and headed down front as the aisle began filling with people.

Spike had already vanished, his guitar and amp gone. The rest of the Skylarks were milling around the stage, taking sips of water and breaking down their gear.

Sadie approached George, whom she'd met once or twice before. He was the band's rhythm guitarist and his wife sometimes came into the Antique Mine looking for quilts to add to her collection.

"Great set, George!" She gave him an enthusiastic thumbs-up. "I haven't heard some of those old hymns in ages."

"Thanks, Sadie!" He removed a bandanna from his back pocket and wiped his bald head. "I felt like we were on fire for a few of them if I do say so myself."

"You all sounded great," she replied. "Spike was especially good. Was that a new guitar he's got?"

"You mean his 'baby'?" George laughed, tucking his bandanna back in his pocket. "Yes, that's the culmination of a lifelong dream—a 1953 Les Paul Gibson Goldtop. The Holy Grail for some of us musicians. So far he won't even let me touch it."

"Why not?" Sadie's heart dropped in her chest. She already knew the answer.

"Are you kidding? It probably cost more than my car!" George shook his head, putting his guitar back in its case. "Rare and valuable at the same time. You could've knocked me over with a feather when I saw it."

Sadie ignored the sinking feeling in her stomach. "Well, maybe you'll have the chance to play it someday."

"That would be nice!" George hefted his guitar case and smiled at Sadie. "Great to talk to you again, Sadie. Glad you enjoyed the show."

She nodded and thanked him once more and then trudged back up the aisle.

Edwin was waiting, and as she approached, he offered her his arm. "Are you sure you're okay?" he murmured as they walked toward the door. "You seem quiet."

"I'll tell you in a moment," she replied, focused on the social niceties—waving, saying hello, making familiar small talk with her acquaintances while Edwin walked beside her, following suit.

It was important for Edwin to take a few moments at these functions to meet and greet people. This was especially important now that they were winding down such a large festival. Even though she usually liked this part best, and even though it was terribly important for Edwin, she didn't enjoy it tonight. Her mind was elsewhere.

They eventually managed to reach Edwin's silver BMW. After he helped her in, buckled his seat belt, and put the car in reverse, he spoke. "Sadie, are you upset with me?"

"Upset? With you?" For a moment, Sadie couldn't fathom what he meant, and she put a placating hand on his arm. "No, not at all." She sighed. "Spike just bought a really expensive guitar from the pawn shop, and he's doing some mighty costly repairs on his shop at the same time. And Ardis told me the repairs aren't covered by his insurance. Do you think it's possible that he worked with our mystery man to steal the watch?"

"Spike? A thief?" Edwin gave her a surprised look. "I don't think so, Sadie. Nothing about Spike suggests he's the kind of person who steals."

"It's just too much of a coincidence," Sadie replied. "First, he's putting thousands of dollars of repairs into his shop after the insurance policy won't pay out. Now, he's purchased a beautiful vintage guitar that cost a small fortune. None of this happened before I found and lost that watch."

Edwin sat in silence for a few moments. Sadie stared out the window, looking out at the vast, clear black sky. Millions of stars dotted the velvety darkness, like a vial of glitter sprinkled across an old black party dress.

"I don't believe for a minute that Spike is a thief," Edwin said firmly. "I admit I don't know for certain, but he is one of us, so I'm going to give him the benefit of the doubt."

Sadie pressed her hand over his, affection washing over her like a wave. "I feel the same way." She shook her head. Spike was not a Silver Peak native, but she had known him a long time. She knew his history, knew him to be a man of character who had known tragedy and loss and still wore it on his face.

Purchasing an expensive instrument like the guitar seemed out of character for him, but at the same time, was it unreasonable that an accomplished musician would be drawn to an instrument of such caliber? And if it helped lift the burden of sorrow he still seemed to carry, how could she begrudge him that?

Edwin smiled at her, his eyes twinkling in the dim light of the car, before he switched his attention back to the road. "On the other hand, I do think it's likely that Spike would help a friend in need, and that it's possible that the friend could lead him astray."

Sadie nodded, thinking of Robert Smith.

Edwin pulled up into Sadie's driveway, and she could see Hank in the front window, his yellow face showing between the lace curtains. Sadie kissed Edwin good night, turning down his offer to walk her to the front porch. The air had turned noticeably colder, driven by a biting wind, and she hated for him to leave the warmth of the car, even for a moment.

She dashed inside, letting Hank wander out into the darkness of the yard before they went to bed. As she opened the door for him, her cell phone rang.

"Hello?" she asked, plucking blond dog hairs from her scarf.

"Hi, Sadie? It's Jack Fitzgerald. I saw you at the gospel service, but you got away before I could speak to you."

"I'm sorry I missed you, Jack." Sadie glanced outside to see if Hank was okay. He was sniffing the ground, wagging his tail. "How are you?"

"I'm fine. Listen, we found something tonight on the train that you'll be interested in."

"Oh?" Sadie's pulse quickened. Had the missing watch been found after all? "What was it?"

"I found a tub of your missing coffee mugs."

Disappointment, then astonishment flared within Sadie. "Are you sure?"

After seeing them displayed so prominently in Darcy Burke's wedding photos, she had already given them a mental kiss goodbye. Yet apparently they were waiting for her at the station.

"Yes. It's the funniest thing. I know I checked that train a million times, looking for them. I thought they'd been pushed under a seat. Well, last night I was closing things up, and I saw them sitting on the back platform of the caboose. I am so sorry, Sadie. I don't know how I overlooked them."

She could certainly enlighten him on that score, but somehow she just couldn't bring herself to tell him that Darcy had taken them. Sadie wondered again how he could have missed them at Darcy's reception, but she knew that many men—her beloved late husband, T.R., included—could look right past the dishes because their eyes were on the food. "Don't worry, Jack. Do you mind if I pick them up over the weekend?"

"Absolutely. In fact, do you want me to deliver them to you? I can do that as soon as the festival is over." Jack's voice sounded eagerly placating, as though he still felt he had to make amends.

"Don't worry, Jack. I appreciate the offer, but I'll come fetch them. If for no other reason than to see that beautiful train once more." The moment she found the watch flashed through Sadie's memory, and she asked, "Speaking of the train, did you ever figure out why the lights went out that night?"

"Oh yeah." Jack chuckled. "We blew a fuse when Darcy plugged in the coffeemaker as we were pulling into the station."

"Why was she plugging it in? Wasn't the beverage service over?" Sadie puzzled out loud.

"It was, but we clean the coffeemakers by running vinegar and water through them at the end of the evening. She was starting that process when the fuse blew."

"What an unlucky coincidence! Well, I hope you can avoid it in the future."

"Yeah, it should be an easy fix. Well—"

"Jack, can I ask you one more question?"

He paused for a moment, but said, "Sure, Sadie."

When she'd called him at Darcy's wedding, she'd forgotten to ask this question, but the thought of Spike working with the mystery man to steal the watch had brought it back to the forefront of her mind.

"On that seating chart you gave me, the seat next to mine was empty, but there was definitely a man sitting next to me that night."

"Really?" She could hear Jack shuffling some papers. "We were very careful about our ticket sales. If I remember right, that seat was sold, but then the day before the event, the buyer had to return the ticket. On such short notice, we didn't sell it again. That seat should have been empty."

Sadie forced a laugh. "Well, I guess you've already had your first stowaway!"

Jack's voice disappeared for a moment, and she could barely hear muffled sounds of conversation between Jack and someone else. "I've got to run, Sadie," he finally said clearly, "but those mugs are here waiting for you."

Hank began pawing at the door. "I'll be by soon."

After she hung up, she let Hank in and poured out a bowlful of food for him. Then she ate one of the blueberry scones Jane had dropped by the shop earlier that week and walked upstairs.

As she changed into her sturdy flannel pajamas, she thought over Jack's explanation for the blown fuse. It was most likely that the lights had gone out by accident, a quirk of timing. She supposed it was just as possible that Darcy had known the fuse would blow and had done it deliberately to cloak the train in darkness while the theft took place, but Sadie found that a little far-fetched. So much for her heist theory.

She shuffled over to grab her bedroom slippers and whistled for Hank, who bounded up the stairs and settled onto his cushion with a contented snort. Then she settled into bed with her scone and warm milk.

More interesting was the confirmation that her mystery man had sneaked aboard the train, probably for the sole purpose of finding the watch. But how had he known about it? Was he working with Darcy, who had learned about it through family legend?

And, try as she might, she still couldn't rid her mind of the image of Spike playing that glittering new guitar. She needed to know if he'd been involved, even innocently.

As with her conversation with Natty, this one would take a great deal of finesse.

The next day dawned rosy and bright. Frost on the windowpanes sparkled in the sun. Winter would soon set in with a vengeance, Sadie reflected as she drove to work in her Tahoe, her heater working overtime to compensate for the morning chill. It really was a good thing that Spike was getting his roof done now, before the winter snows started in earnest. As curious as Sadie was about where he'd gotten the money, at least he was putting it to good use.

As she stopped at an intersection in town, a familiar car caught her eye. The last time she had seen this vehicle, the driver had burned rubber to get away from her.

Darcy Burke. Or Darcy…? Sadie realized she didn't know Darcy's married name.

Sadie waited and watched as the light turned green. Darcy turned toward the train station. Was she really headed back?

Sadie glanced down at her watch. It was still early enough that a quick side trip wouldn't delay her opening the Antique Mine. She flicked on her blinker and eased over, and when the light turned, she drove toward the station.

She hung back as the little hatchback disappeared from view, not wanting to startle Darcy again. When Sadie finally reached the parking lot, Darcy's hatchback was wide open, and a quick glance showed a familiar plastic tub and cardboard box had been stuffed inside.

Sadie parked beside Darcy's car and switched off the ignition. She scanned the station parking lot and the grounds just beyond, but there was no sign of the brunette.

Sadie waited, sipping patiently on her coffee until a figure clad in a puffy down jacket darted out of the shelter beside the train. The figure hustled back to the parking lot as quickly as she could without breaking into a run.

Sadie opened her car door and slipped out. She didn't shut the door completely, not wanting to draw attention to herself. Darcy hadn't looked up yet or noticed Sadie's car.

As Darcy rushed toward her car, her head bowed against the frosty morning air, Sadie waited until the young woman was only a few feet away before she spoke.

"Hello, Darcy." Her breath made little clouds in the still morning air.

Darcy skidded to a stop, her brown eyes huge in her pale face.

19

"Mrs. Speers!" Darcy gasped. Before Sadie could say anything, Darcy burst into speech. "*Please* don't call the sheriff. I brought all the cups and tea set back. See? I'm returning the last of them now." She pointed toward her hatchback.

Sadie held up a hand, palm out. "Don't worry, Darcy. I'm not calling the police. I saw the tea set and the mugs in the wedding pictures that Mrs. Sweeting took." She took a step closer to Darcy and patted her back. "I knew you had them."

Darcy's eyes filled with tears. "What?"

"At first we thought they'd just been misplaced," Sadie replied. "Then when I saw the photos, I knew you had taken them to use in your wedding. If you'd have asked me, I would have let you borrow them. In fact, I would have let you borrow more. I have all kinds of 1930s-era goodies in my store."

"I didn't think you'd let me borrow anything after I broke that mug. I saw your face and how upset you were." Two tears ran down Darcy's face. "Why didn't you call the police? I would have. You didn't know whether I was returning them or not. For all you knew, I had stolen them."

Sadie shrugged. "You're right, I didn't know for sure. I think I just assumed that, if you needed them that badly, they were meant for you to use. I knew how much you loved antiques from that era and that they would be well taken care of and cherished." She remembered the moment Darcy broke the mug on the train, and how distraught the young woman had been. "I'm sorry if I looked upset on the train when the mug fell and broke. It's always a little upsetting to see a beautiful antique break, but it was only one mug. I'm sorry if you thought I was angry. The truth is I'd forgotten all about it until you mentioned it just now."

Darcy began crying in earnest. "I feel awful," she howled. "When I took them, I was just thinking of myself. We had no money for the wedding. My husband and I are both broke, but I wanted to have a special day just the same. So that night, after the party, instead of taking everything to be cleaned, I took the mugs and hot chocolate set with me."

Sadie patted Darcy's back and let her cry. Sometimes, a good cry was worth more than anything in the world.

"When...when I saw you the next day, I knew I'd never be able to look you in the eye. So I took off, and I quit my job. Uncle Jack was so upset. I'm so sorry, Mrs. Speers. I hope I can repay the damage I've done."

"There's no harm done, none at all," Sadie murmured, keeping her voice calm and soothing. "I don't want you to look back on your special day with regret. I want you to be able to look at those wedding pictures and remember the happiest day of your life—without worrying that you borrowed a few items without asking."

Darcy gave a sputtering little laugh, wiping her eyes with the back of her gloved hands. "I don't think that's possible. I'll always feel guilty about this." She looked at Sadie, her eyes reddened and slightly swollen. "But thank you for being so cool about it, Mrs. Speers."

Sadie nodded and opened the door to her Tahoe. She reached inside and grasped a box of Kleenex that she kept in the center console.

"Here." She handed Darcy the box. Darcy muttered her thanks and drew out a few tissues.

"So how did the wedding turn out?" Sadie asked, smiling.

Darcy gave a short, rueful laugh followed by a blissful sigh. "Perfect." She was nearly glowing.

Sadie looked at Darcy for a few seconds, her face alight with the hope and joy of her future, and made a decision.

"Darcy, I want you to have the things you borrowed. Think of it as a wedding gift from me."

Darcy paused in the middle of blowing her nose, her wide brown eyes growing larger as she gazed at Sadie. "What?"

"I want you to have them. I know you will give them a good home. If you have too many of the mugs, bring them by the Antique Mine and I'll sell them on consignment." Sadie gave her a warm smile. This was the right thing to do.

"I don't know what to say, Mrs. Speers. You are one in a million." Darcy wiped her eyes and wadded the used tissues in her pocket. "My husband and I are starting a little coffeehouse in our hometown. I'd be pleased to use the mugs for our customers. I'd put the hot chocolate set on display in a place of honor."

Sadie's heart glowed and she wrapped her arms around Darcy, giving her an impulsive squeeze. "That sounds wonderful! What a lovely way to start your new business. Little unique flourishes like that will help you stand apart from the crowd."

"I don't know what to say, other than thank you." Darcy squeezed her back. "Thank you so very, very much."

"You are more than welcome. Let me know when you open. I'll stop by."

Darcy chuckled. "Okay. I promise to send an e-mail to the Antique Mine when we are open for business."

"There's another tub of mugs in the station," Sadie said. "Come with me. We'll go in together and grab it."

As they walked across the frosted grass, Sadie seized the opportunity to put her mind at rest about one more detail. "Darcy, do you know someone named Spike Harris?"

"That doesn't ring a bell," Darcy said, shrugging. "Why?"

"He owns the music shop downtown and has a great band called the Skylarks. I—uh, I thought you could ask him to come out and play a set in your coffeehouse."

"Oh. Maybe I will." Darcy gave her an uncertain smile.

Sadie thought a moment. So far, she knew that the Elliotts weren't involved. Spike might have been involved. She felt certain her mystery man was involved. And now was her chance to ask Darcy about their conversation that night.

"There's one other person I want to ask you about. The man sitting beside me on the train—I never caught his name, and later, he disappeared. I think someone saw him ask you something."

"Oh yeah." She rolled her eyes. "He asked me out on a date, but I told him I was engaged. He was a little old for me anyway, but I didn't say that."

"Did he tell you his name?"

"Yeah, I think so. Billy? Ricky? Something like that."

Sadie's heart started to pound. "Robbie?"

Darcy beamed at her. "Yeah, that was it! He said his name was Robbie, and he was new in town."

20

Darcy paused, biting her lip. "I was actually carrying those mugs out to my car when he approached me. I was more concerned about stashing them in my trunk without getting caught than I was about anything he might have to say to me. Besides, even if I weren't engaged, I would never date a man who wore a wig." She giggled.

Sadie stared at her. All she could manage to say was, "A wig?"

"Yeah, he took off his hat when he saw me, and the wig slipped."

Robbie? The Robert Smith she knew?

A wig. Fake glasses. Why such an elaborate disguise? Was it just part of his vintage costuming?

Or was it part of the heist, if in fact there was one? And was that why he'd pretended not to know her when they'd met at Spike's apartment? Why he'd sneaked onto the train?

At least this accounted for the strange sense of familiarity she'd felt the first few times she'd seen him. It wasn't just his resemblance to Collin Malloy. She'd sat by him on the train, talked to him. Looked into those blue eyes.

Sadie swallowed. "I see. I just wondered if you knew him personally. I'm glad you remembered his name, though. I'm sure you were distracted by cleaning up."

"Yeah, especially after I blew that fuse. I was so sure that Uncle Jack would be angry."

So the blown fuse was an accident, and Robert Smith, Spike's good friend, was her mysterious disappearing seatmate.

Sadie snapped off her train of thought. It would do absolutely no good to brood about Spike right now. The most important thing was helping Darcy retrieve the mugs. Once they were packed safely in the trunk of Darcy's little hatchback, Sadie could put the incident out of her mind.

She pushed open the door of the station, and Darcy followed her inside. She entered the office and began to lift the box, but Darcy stopped her.

"Let me do it. It's kinda heavy."

Sadie nodded and permitted the young woman to heft the box. Then she led the way back to Darcy's car, holding the doors open for her and helping her slide the box securely into the back.

"Thank you again." Darcy hugged Sadie once more and climbed into the driver's seat. "Bye, Mrs. Speers. Hope to see you again soon."

Sadie waved as Darcy circled the parking lot and left.

As she climbed back into the Tahoe, her phone began ringing. "Hello?"

"Mom, where are you?" Alice's curiosity came through her voice. "You aren't at the Antique Mine yet. Are you out investigating?" Her tone turned teasing.

Sadie laughed and pressed the hands-free button on her console, then turned on the ignition. "Maybe just a little. I had an errand to run. What's up?"

"Nothing. I just wanted to talk to you before tonight." Alice sighed, her breath crackling into the speaker. "Mom, I am so nervous. This is worse than when I first started dating as a teenager."

Sadie eased the Tahoe onto the main road. "There's nothing to worry about." She'd pushed Alice's date to the back of her mind as she tackled the issues of Natty Flats, the Elliotts, and Darcy, whose new last name Sadie had somehow forgotten to ask. Now Alice's nervousness snapped her back to the present, triggering all her maternal instincts. "Just go and have a good time. At the very least, you'll enjoy some good music."

"I suppose. Are you coming with Edwin? Can I ride with you?" Usually when Alice's questions piled on top of each other, she was dealing with the children while she talked.

"Yes to both." Sadie smiled. "Give the kids my love. Are you taking them to their dad's?"

"We're on the way out the door now." A commotion of voices, rustling, and the thumping of shoes and doors in the background signaled that Alice was probably shooing the kids toward the car.

"Give their dad my love too." Sadie didn't understand the reasons Cliff had left Alice, but in her mind, he was still her son-in-law, as well as her grandchildren's father.

"Okay, I will." Alice's voice grew muffled. The muted sounds of car doors opening and shutting signaled the end of the conversation. "See you tonight!" Alice said, then hung up.

Sadie gave her full attention to the road. She couldn't shake the uneasiness that Alice's reminder about her date had ignited in her soul. Had she really caught Alice's nerves? Was she worried about tonight?

No, it was her questions about Spike—and Robert—that were gnawing at her. Though some of her other questions were resolved, his remained unanswered. What if Spike had helped Robert steal the watch, and he was now living off part of the proceeds? Robert had worn a disguise on the train, and disappeared immediately after she lost the watch. Now he was staying with Spike, who suddenly had enough money to pay for roof repairs and a rare guitar. The situation was just too coincidental.

As she neared the shop, the ringing blows from the roofer's hammers and nail guns crashed through the morning air, not dulled in the least by her rolled-up windows and the music on her radio. Sadie sighed.

There had to be another explanation. There simply had to be.

Alice fidgeted in the backseat as Edwin drove toward town. "Thanks so much for letting me catch a ride with you."

"Of course," Edwin responded. "It's not every day that I get to take *two* lovely ladies to a dance."

Sadie turned in her seat, giving her daughter a bracing smile. "You look beautiful."

She really did. Alice wore a lovely flowered dress, and her hair had been slightly curled, giving her normally practical daughter a distinctly romantic look.

"I feel ridiculous. Sitting back here with the two of you up front makes me feel like a teenager again." Alice looked out the window.

"Stepping out of our comfort zone and making changes is always uncomfortable," Sadie reminded her. "Do you really want to date again?"

"Yes and no. I miss having someone to share my life with, but I am not at all sure I'm ready to take this step." Alice sighed. "There's nothing to do now but go through with it."

Sadie nodded and faced forward again. If Alice knew her date in person and hadn't only chatted with him online, things might be easier. If she already knew him, perhaps this next step in their relationship would seem less awkward and more organic.

She couldn't say that out loud, of course. Alice felt nervous enough already. She needed all the support she could get.

Edwin swung the car into the high school parking lot. The square dance was being held in the gym, and the lights from the building streamed out into the dark night. A steady trickle of couples wandered from the lot to the building, some in full square-dance regalia and some more conservatively dressed.

Edwin pulled the car into a spot and parked. As he got out, Sadie turned back to her daughter. "How will you know if your date is here?"

"I promised to text him once I arrived." Alice pulled her phone out of her purse as Edwin opened her door.

Sadie shook her head, for this was another entirely modern addition to the dating scene. Edwin opened her car door and offered his arm. She was glad to know that old-fashioned chivalry lived on in Edwin. She smiled up at him, and followed Alice inside, her arm tucked into the crook of Edwin's elbow.

As they entered the gym, the sound of a lively two-step cascaded over them. The Skylarks were in fine form, and Spike lit into an ornate and well-played guitar solo as they walked in the door.

Alice tucked her phone into her purse and shrugged out of her coat. "He's not here yet," she called to her mother, cupping her hands around her mouth so she could be heard above the din.

Sadie nodded and allowed Edwin to help her out of her coat. Then he draped Alice's coat over his arm as well and took both garments over to the coat check.

Sadie gave her full attention to the dancers, swirling around as George called the figures. She nodded to the beat, tapping her foot, and turned toward the stage.

Robert Smith stood next to Spike, his upright bass in his hands.

21

Alice scanned the crowd, her phone glowing in her hand. "He says he's here," she muttered. "I don't see him yet, though."

At that moment, a somewhat short balding man came up behind Alice. Sadie opened her mouth to say something, but the man gave her an impish grin and put his finger to his lips. Then, with a wink, he tapped Alice's shoulder.

"Surprise!" he hollered, his voice so loud that it could be heard above the band and the stomping dancers' feet.

Alice jumped and turned around. "Arthur!" she gasped. From her expression, Sadie could tell that her daughter was more taken aback than pleased. "You startled me."

"Sorry." Arthur chuckled. "You're even prettier in person than on your profile. I'm a lucky guy tonight!"

Alice gave a weak smile. "Arthur, this is my mother, Sadie Speers." She indicated Sadie with a wave of her hand.

"Pleased to meet you!" Arthur effused. He squeezed Sadie's hand in a damp grip, beaming from ear to ear.

"You too."

Sadie's heart lurched. Arthur seemed to be overcompensating for his nerves. His damp hands and overly enthusiastic behavior reminded her of a puppy trying to please its master.

Unfortunately, Alice had never liked overly enthusiastic anything. She was calmness personified. Why, once she got old enough to watch *Gone with the Wind*, she'd reacted to Rhett kissing Scarlett with a single word: *"Gross."*

"The night is young, and we aren't getting any younger ourselves." Arthur turned to Alice with a bow. "Shall we?"

Casting a last, desperate look at her mother, Alice allowed herself to be piloted out onto the dance floor.

Edwin strolled up as they departed, watching the pair with keen interest. "I take it that's Alice's date?"

"Yes. That's Arthur." Sadie sighed. "It's already a disaster."

Edwin raised his eyebrows but said nothing. They watched as Arthur and Alice joined a square. At length, he muttered, "He can dance, at least."

"Their personalities don't suit," Sadie replied, engrossed in memories of Alice when she was a newlywed and blissfully happy. "I want her to find someone who makes her feel content."

Edwin patted her shoulder and they stood in silence, watching the dancers whirl by. It felt good to have Edwin there beside her, sharing in her disappointment as her daughter suffered through the dance. Sharing the burden was nice, even if Alice was having a bad time of it.

"Sadie!" Roz appeared and gave Sadie a quick hug. Roscoe ambled up behind her, offering his hand to Edwin. "I feel like it's been ages! Any exciting developments?"

"A few." That was an understatement, but it would take lunch at Arbuckle's to explain everything to her best friend. "Let's get together soon for a recap."

"Perfect. Once the festival is over, we'll have time to breathe." Roz lifted an eyebrow at her as though trying to read her mind, then followed Sadie's gaze to the dance floor.

Sadie nodded at the dancers. "Alice has a date. It doesn't seem to be going well."

Roz scanned the crowd. "Oh dear," she breathed, as Arthur spun Alice around like a windmill. "Poor Alice."

Sadie glanced up at the stage. Spike had noticed Alice's date, and his eyes kept flicking toward her as she danced. Sadie shook her head slowly. She could see how Spike felt about her daughter, but Alice seemed oblivious to his feelings, and Spike's normally retiring demeanor prevented him from doing anything beyond admiring her from afar.

George called the final figure, and the music ended with a flourish. Alice curtsied gracefully and then walked off the dance floor, not allowing Arthur to lead her. Arthur trailed behind, pulling a large handkerchief from his pocket to wipe the sweat from his brow.

Alice made a beeline straight for Sadie. When she got close enough that she could speak and be heard, she called, "Mom, do you need something?"

The pleading look in her daughter's eyes spoke volumes. Alice needed rescue.

"Yes. I am so sorry to take you away from the dance, but I snagged my hem as we walked in." Sadie balled up the fabric of her skirt in her right hand. "Can you help me pin it so it hangs straight?"

"Of course." Alice turned to Arthur. "Excuse us, won't you?"

They hurried toward the ladies' room at the corner of the gym. A line stretched out the door and wound down one side of the gym. Alice groaned in frustration.

"Here, follow me," Sadie said.

She drew Alice over to a dark corner off the stage, where the music was loud but they couldn't be seen.

Alice sagged as they gained the privacy of the darkened niche. "This was a bad idea. I want to leave, but I'm stuck here because I rode with you."

Sadie drew Alice close for a hug. "Don't worry about it. Everyone has a bad date now and then."

As she embraced her daughter, she caught a glimpse of Spike out of the corner of her eye. The Skylarks were winding up the song, and soon everything would fall quiet as they reached the end.

"At least you tried."

Alice leaned back, fanning her reddened cheeks with the tips of her fingers. "Yeah, but how do I get out of it now?"

"We'll make some excuse and then go. I'll ask Edwin to take us home."

The last word echoed off the walls of their little niche, and Spike turned, spying them both. The other Skylarks began putting their instruments aside, and George called into the microphone, "Now we'll have a short break. See y'all in fifteen!"

Spike set his flashy guitar on a stand and walked toward them.

Alice turned, completely unaware of Spike's approach. "Let's go now, between sets," she called. She walked briskly across the gym floor, expertly weaving her way in and out of the couples that were drifting off the dance floor.

Spike halted and stuck his hands in the pockets of his worn leather jacket. Sadie started to reach out to him, but something told her that Spike wouldn't relish the thought of making polite conversation at this moment. Alice was waiting for her too.

She followed Alice's path across the dance floor, drawing close to Edwin. "Can you take us home?" she asked, fixing him with an "I will tell you later" look.

Edwin glanced between Sadie and Alice, who was making apologies to her overly enthusiastic date. He nodded. "I'll go get our coats." He walked off without any further delay.

Sadie made her good-byes to Arthur, Roz, and Roscoe. Roz gave her a knowing glance but wisely stayed mum about any suspicions she had.

About halfway to Sadie's house, Alice finally spoke from the back of the car. "I'm so sorry I cut your date short."

Edwin smiled into the rearview mirror. "Don't worry, Alice. I'm sure your mom will let me ask her out again."

They all laughed, a magical sound that broke the tension that had been simmering all evening.

"Mom," Alice said, "do you mind if I stay with you tonight? With the kids gone, I'd rather not go home to an empty house tonight."

"Of course. We can make hot cocoa and watch a movie." Sadie smiled at the thought of getting to spend some true quality time with her daughter.

"I just want to soak in a warm bath, and then go to bed." Alice yawned.

"You can even have your old room," Sadie assured her.

"Well, if you don't get to watch old movies tonight, don't forget about the movie festival tomorrow," Edwin reminded them. "It's the last big event of the week."

"What are they showing?" Alice's voice sounded tired.

"A Collin Malloy musical, *Merrily We Roll*. Some other early movies, shorts, newsreels. Stuff from the early 1930s." Edwin deftly steered the car into the driveway. "I'd be happy to take you two again."

"I think I'll pass," Alice said with a smile. "But thanks, Edwin."

Alice let herself out of the car and quickly hurried up the path to the house. She let herself inside and Hank slipped through the door out into the yard.

As Sadie watched her daughter's swift flight indoors, she heaved a sigh. "Edwin, I know someone who's in love with Alice."

"Yes, but I don't think Arthur's going to get another chance." Edwin unbuckled his seat belt and moved to open his door.

Sadie put a hand on his arm. "It's Spike."

Edwin turned toward her, his dark eyes pools of concern in the dim light. "Are you sure?"

"I've known for a while." She sagged against the seat. "But I'm not sure he'll ever let her know, and I don't think it's my place to tell her."

"Do you still think that Spike had something to do with the pocket watch?" Edwin took her hand in his.

Again, it struck her how nice it was to be able to share these fears with him. She could always call Roz, of course. Roz would listen and give advice and act as a sounding board. But when all was said and done, Roz was a friend, not a partner.

"I can't shake the feeling he might have. Unless my information is completely wrong, and I don't believe it is, my mysterious seatmate is Robert Smith, the Collin Malloy lookalike who's staying with Spike. How could he not be involved? It's time for me to talk to him about it. Past time, in fact." She sighed.

Edwin pressed her hand. "I often had to make tough decisions when it came to some cases," he responded quietly. "But I followed through and made those calls even when it was difficult. Do you want me to come along?"

"No. It will be easier if it's just the two of us. I don't want Spike to feel ganged up on." She squeezed his hand in return. "Thank you, Edwin. I've been thinking all evening that it's wonderful to be able to share all of this with you. I really appreciate your support."

She leaned forward and pecked his cheek. Hank trotted up to the car and barked excitedly, his tail wagging back and forth in the light flooding the yard from the headlights.

Sadie chuckled. "I had better go. I have a dog and a daughter waiting."

Edwin kissed her cheek. "I'll see you to the door."

After Edwin accompanied her to the porch, Sadie watched as he swung his car around and drove off into the night, the taillights of his car glowing red in the darkness.

Upstairs, the sound of rushing water signaled that Alice was making good on her wish to take a warm bath. Hank chewed on an old rawhide bone that he'd kept hidden indoors for over a week now.

Sadie headed to the kitchen to make hot cocoa. Despite the warm coziness of her home, she shivered. If only she could be certain of Spike without having to confront him. Unfortunately, she reflected as she began warming milk in the saucepan, such certainty was impossible. She'd chased down Natty Flats with a peace offering of coffee and pie and a hope that he'd open up to her and Sara. She'd given Darcy boxes of antique mugs. She'd confronted Grace Elliott and even hinted that she suspected them of fraud.

Spike and Robert Smith were the only likely candidates left. If Spike hadn't been a friend, and if she didn't know about his feelings for Alice, she would have said something by now.

Sadie poured cocoa powder into the milk, stirring it as it simmered.

There was no need to be afraid and every reason to ask Spike for the truth.

22

Sadie climbed the steps to Spike's apartment. The roofers, despite the need to have the repairs done quickly, weren't working on Saturday, so at least she would be able to hear herself think. She balanced three cups of coffee from Arbuckle's in a cardboard tray, taking care not to slosh them around too much as she went up the stairs.

She shifted the tray to one hand and rapped on Spike's door. Surely he would be up by now; his store would be open for business in an hour. As she waited, she said a silent prayer for strength and grace.

After a brief pause, Spike opened the door. He was dressed casually in a long-sleeved T-shirt, faded blue jeans, and wooly socks. Seeing Spike without his trusty leather jacket and without the protection of his shoes made him seem even more vulnerable.

Sadie gave him a warm smile and lifted the tray of coffee. "Hi, Spike. Do you mind if I come in? I need to talk to you."

"Um, sure." Spike opened the door wider. "Sorry, the place is a mess."

Sadie stifled a laugh, because her idea of a mess and Spike's idea of a mess apparently were two very different things.

The living room was airy and pin-neat, and Spike had furnished it with a 1940s-vintage overstuffed sofa and chair, as well as tasteful Art Deco touches, such as the pristine end tables and coffee table that accompanied them. The walls carried on the vintage theme, with beautiful Art Deco–framed landscape photographs by Ansel Adams arranged in neat patterns on one side of the room, and a few original oil paintings in a colorful abstract style on the other. Sadie felt sure she knew the artist but couldn't think of her name. An entire end wall was taken up with shelves that contained books of every kind and era, and a beautiful orange tiger cat occupied the top of the couch back, staring lazily out the large window. It turned its head for a moment to study Sadie with languid eyes and then turned back to the window.

For a moment, all Sadie could think about was where he had found all these amazing pieces, since she knew he hadn't gotten them from the Antique Mine. Perhaps they stemmed from his time in Los Angeles as a successful studio musician.

Spike gestured for her to take a seat on the couch. A book with a bookmark in it, a copy of *Guitar Player Magazine*, and a *Rolling Stone* were on the coffee table, and a violin case tucked in next to the door constituted the only things that could possibly be construed as a "mess." Sadie slid the magazines to one side to make room for the coffee cups she'd brought along. "I realize it's a little rude to burst in on you like this, so I brought coffee to make up for it."

"Thanks. I was going to brew a pot anyway, but this is even better." He sat on a chair opposite her and ruffled his hand through his hair. "You brought three cups…"

"I thought Robbie might still be here, and I didn't want him to feel left out."

"He got a call last night for an early interview today in Denver, so he drove there after the show."

"Oh, that's too bad. The Skylarks were fantastic last night, and at the gospel sing, and I wanted to tell you both how much I enjoyed both shows."

Spike smiled. "Thanks. Robbie'll be back tonight, so I can let him know." He sipped at his coffee.

"Sounds good." She took a drink of her coffee. It calmed her nerves to have some way to occupy her hands. "How long have you known Robbie?"

"Robbie and I were session musicians together in LA." Spike eyed her over the rim of his cup. "When I first met him, he was working as an actor and a magician. He was kind of a one-man show. Talented in music, acting, magic—you name it."

"So he's a good friend." Sadie sipped her coffee slowly, hoping Spike would keep talking.

He shrugged. "Yeah. I guess you could say that. Known him for a long time. He's a good guy." Spike set down his coffee, troubled eyes studying her. "Look, Sadie, what are you really here to talk about?"

"I actually wanted to speak with you about the night we were on the train."

Spike gave her a puzzled look. "Oh, okay. Um, what about it?"

Sadie took a deep breath and dived in. "That night I found a diamond pocket watch tucked into the cushion of my train seat. While I was holding it, trying to get a closer look, the man sitting next to me saw it too. I was going to turn it in to the train conductor, but the lights went out. When they came back on, the watch was gone." Her heart beat strangely in her chest, and she took a deep, calming breath.

"The pocket watch is the one that was meant to be given to Collin Malloy, the opera star, by the people of Silver Peak back in 1931. Through a strange set of circumstances, which I'm just starting to piece together, it came to be concealed on the train. No one knew it was there, Spike, except a few people, if that."

"The same watch that's been in the paper? There's some sort of treasure hunt for it, right?" Spike seemed nonchalant, as if still puzzled what this conversation had to do with him. If he had taken the watch or been in on the theft, she would have expected him to seem more nervous.

Sadie set her coffee down and folded her hands together. "The man sitting next to me was Robbie, Spike. He was in disguise. And he didn't buy a ticket; he snuck onto the train. It's just odd that Robbie went to such lengths to get on the train without being recognized, saw the watch, and then a few minutes later the watch disappeared. Robbie is staying with you, and I saw the repairs you're doing on your shop, and your new guitar—"

"Hang on." Spike stood up. "Robbie's a friend, and I haven't seen anything like a diamond pocket watch on him. He hasn't said anything to me about it. Would a guy who stole an expensive watch be looking for a job as a session musician in Denver?"

"I understand he's your friend," she said quietly, "but you have to admit it looks suspicious. He had the perfect opportunity to take the watch, and suddenly you can afford a brand-new roof and a rare guitar."

Spike sagged against the wall and gave her an incredulous look. "Robbie didn't give me that money." He heaved a deep, shuddering breath. "The money came from my mother-in-law. She passed away recently."

Sadie's breath caught in her throat. "I'm so sorry."

"She left me the money because it belonged to my wife." He averted his gaze and stared at a fixed point on the wall opposite him. "My mother-in-law and I barely spoke after Kim and Wendy died. We were too sharp a reminder to each other of what we'd lost." He rubbed a hand over the stubble of beard growth on his chin.

Sadie felt tears prickle in the back of her eyes.

"When she passed away, she left her money to me. I think it was one last way to say she didn't blame me." He lifted his head and fixed Sadie with a strong, certain gaze. "Robbie has always been there for me. In fact, he performed as a magician at Wendy's last birthday party. Robbie knew about the wreck. He knew that when Carol—that was my mother-in-law—died, she willed the money to me. He's a good guy. A bit of a gambler, kind of reckless, but not a thief."

Sadie nodded slowly. She believed that Spike felt this strongly about his friend, and it spoke well of Spike to be so loyal.

Spike hunched over, shoving his hands in the pockets of his jeans. "Robbie came to Silver Peak because he finished a tour on the cast of a traveling play and had a job prospect in Denver. We hadn't seen each other in a while, so I invited him to stay. He certainly didn't come to steal a watch."

"I understand." Sadie's face warmed under Spike's stare. This was as far as this conversation could go. She didn't want to risk offending Spike even more and hurting their friendship. She grabbed her coffee cup from the table. "I guess I'll see you later, Spike."

"Sure." Spike walked with her to the door. As his hand rested on the knob, he stopped for a long moment. He seemed to be struggling with something, and finally he turned toward her. "Look, Robbie's not straight as an arrow. He's done some gambling in the past, gotten into debt. But he's trying to make a fresh start—that's why he left LA and why he's looking for work elsewhere."

Sadie nodded. "Thanks, Spike. You're a good man."

He ducked his head as though her comment embarrassed him. As she stepped onto the threshold, he shut the door firmly behind her.

Sadie sagged for a moment against the banister, her strength diminishing. Poor Spike. For his sake she hoped his friend wasn't a thief, but she couldn't believe it herself.

She trudged down the steps and noticed a box sitting outside the Dumpster that sat behind Spike's building. That was odd. After seeing Spike's apartment, it seemed out of character for him to dispose of trash in such a careless manner. Sadie walked over to take a closer look, intending to throw the box into the Dumpster rather than leave it on the ground.

The cardboard was squashed, crumpled, and filled with detritus—old takeout containers, T-shirts with holes worn at the seams, a broken guitar string, and an assortment of guitar picks cut from old credit cards. She glanced around to see if anyone might be watching, then fitted the card pieces together like a puzzle, and the original owner's name became clear: Robert Smith.

Sadie looked around, arguing with herself. Digging through Robert Smith's trash felt like crossing some sort of line, but maybe she could learn more about him. She didn't see anyone nearby who might spot her, so she shifted through the box's contents and found a large fake mustache. She looked at it sadly, remembering it clearly from when it adorned the mystery man's face. She dropped the mustache and dug down to the bottom of the box, finding a yellowed envelope, addressed in faded, handwritten script. The stamp was interesting. Definitely several decades old.

Sadie drew it out of the box. There appeared to be a letter still inside, and the envelope had been slit open at the top. She scanned the address—it was addressed to John Smith in Los Angeles, California. Robert's father?

Sadie bit her lip, hesitating for a moment before tucking the letter into her jacket pocket. It wasn't stealing if Robert had thrown it away, right? The faded handwriting and unique stamp piqued her interest, and she wanted to know what the letter said. The rest of the box was free of anything of interest, so Sadie threw it into the Dumpster.

Time to open the Antique Mine. She headed across the street. Her confrontation with Spike had completely drained her of energy and cheer. Now she just wanted to go home and climb under the covers for a few hours, with Hank snoring gently at the foot of her bed.

Her phone buzzed, and she switched her coffee cup to her other hand so she could answer it. "Hello?"

"Mom, it's me." Alice's voice sounded tense. "I can't come help at the store today. I have to go to Breckenridge. Theo had an accident."

Sadie stumbled, catching her balance at the last moment as she stepped up on the sidewalk outside her store. "What? What happened? Is he okay?"

"I don't know. All I know is that their dad took them skiing this morning, and Theo fell." Alice's voice broke. "Keep us in prayer, Mom. I'm headed there now."

"Of course." Sadie sat down on the bench outside her store, willing herself to stay calm and collected. "I'll call Julie to take over the store so I can come be with you."

"Don't worry about that yet," Alice said. "I'll call you as soon as I know more." She hung up the phone with a *click*.

Sadie sat, the phone grasped limply in her hand. *Please, God, let Theo be okay.*

23

THE MORNING PASSED IN A STRANGE BLUR. SADIE PERFORMED THE routine tasks of helping customers and straightening the store, but her mind was fixed on Theo and Alice. Would Theo be all right? What had happened?

The noise of the store was muted and hushed, as though everything were wrapped in wool. She prayed and stayed active in the store, and that kept her calm—at least until Alice could phone and give her an update.

She sat, staring out the window, as Marge Ruxton browsed through the shop. Marge was quiet this morning, which was unusual for her. She had a reputation as the town busybody and usually had an opinion on every subject. But for the gift of Marge's silence this morning, Sadie was grateful.

The door opened with a jingle of chimes, and Laura stuck her head inside the shop. "Want some company?"

"I'd love it." Sadie turned to her cousin and smiled.

Laura came into the shop, shutting the door behind her. "You look so downcast. Is everything all right?"

Sadie shook her head. "Theo fell while he was skiing, and Alice left over an hour ago to be with him at the hospital."

Marge, who was browsing over by the potbelly stove, made a *tsking* sound. "You couldn't pay me to ski. It's so dangerous! When you think of all the famous people who've died while skiing—Sonny Bono, Natasha Richardson, Michael Kennedy—well, it's enough to frighten you off the slopes permanently."

Sadie winced. In times of grief or trouble, some people knew just the right thing to say. Others, like Marge, managed to take a difficult situation and make it worse—probably without meaning any harm in the least.

"Theo's an excellent skier and a strong young man. I'm sure he'll be fine."

"Those ski resorts should make people wear helmets," Marge pronounced. "The liability alone—"

"Yes," Sadie interrupted. She couldn't bear to hear anything more about it. God was in control, and she had prayed about it. There was nothing to do but wait.

Laura, probably sensing an argument, abruptly switched their attention to the Collin Malloy display on the wall. "These are neat," she said, walking over to examine the pictures more closely. "I love old photos." She pointed to one of the images. "Who is this? I don't recognize her."

"That's Betty Bright, a starlet in the 1930s," Sadie said. "Doesn't she look adorable?"

Betty Bright's photo was a candid shot of the petite young blonde knitting as she lounged in a director's chair. Sadie had loved the glimpse into an actress's life on-set and hadn't been able to bear leaving it out of the display, especially since the caption on the back of the photo said it was taken on the set of *Merrily We Roll,* the film Betty Bright had made with Collin Malloy.

"Betty Bright. What a lovely name." Laura moved closer to the photo. "You know, women used to knit all the time. It's coming back as a hobby now, but it sure went out of vogue for a while. Funny that she was knitting on a movie set, though. You'd think the big stars would be above that kind of thing."

"You'd think that, but they had to wait around between takes for a long time," Sadie said moving to stand beside Laura. "I've seen photos of Joan Crawford and Myrna Loy knitting on their sets. Of course, Betty Bright was just a starlet and not a major star, but judging by this photo, she was as industrious as the other big-time actresses of her day."

"She's even knitting a sock—something to wear. Not just a blanket or an afghan," Laura said.

Marge sniffed. "Well, I guess I'll be going." Her tone implied disapproval of such frivolous topics.

Sadie sighed as Marge opened the front door and strolled off down the sidewalk.

Laura shrugged. "So are you going to the movies tonight? It's the last big event of the week."

"I planned to, but it depends on how Theo is doing. I may need to make a trip to be with them." Her phone began buzzing insistently. "Oh, thank goodness. It's Alice. Do you mind watching the counter while I take her call?"

"Sure. Give her my love."

Sadie picked up the phone. "Alice? Is everything all right?"

She tried to keep her voice calm as she walked through the store. She didn't have any customers, but she didn't want to sound panicked—that could make Alice feel even worse.

"Theo's fine." Alice sounded happy but teary too. "Just a broken arm."

"Oh, thank the Lord." Sadie leaned against the outside wall of the Antique Mine, relief flooding through her. "I was so worried!"

"I was too." Alice drew a shaky breath. "It could have been so much worse."

"I agree." Now that she was certain Theo was going to be okay, Sadie was able to laugh. "Bring him home. I'll make him some chicken soup."

"We're going to stay here for a couple of days," Alice replied. "I'm staying at a hotel. I want to make sure his cast is on right and won't need any adjustments before we head back to Silver Peak. We should be home Sunday. Then you can spoil him all you want."

"Good. Laura's here with me and sends her love, and so do I. Tell Theo I'll sign his cast when he gets home."

Alice laughed. "I'll tell him. Have fun with Edwin at the movies tonight, Mom." She hung up with a *click*.

Sadie paused for a moment, cradling her phone against her chest, and said a quick prayer of thanksgiving. Theo just had a broken arm, practically a rite of passage for a teenage boy. How mothers with teenage sons survived the sudden adrenaline rushes of emergency room visits, broken limbs, and concussions, she would never know. Alice was such a well-behaved, docile girl, and she had never given Sadie and T.R. a moment's trouble.

"Is Theo all right?" Laura stuck her head out the door.

Sadie gathered her wits about her and walked back into the store. "Theo's fine—just a broken arm. Thank goodness!"

"What a relief."

Sadie finally felt relaxed enough to smile. Nothing would take away her relief right now. Tonight was a night to celebrate. She couldn't wait to go to the movies with Edwin and see her friends.

As she worked the rest of the day, she mulled over the watch's possible fate. She knew that Robert Smith, who looked remarkably like Collin Malloy, had been her seatmate on the train. He had seen the watch. He had helped her when she fell.

At first she had wondered if the theft had been committed by more than one person. The lights going out, someone causing her to stumble, and then the watch disappearing from her hand—it all seemed too elaborate to be attempted by one person. But the more she learned the more she was certain it wasn't a planned heist. Someone had simply taken advantage of the opportunity.

Robert Smith.

Somehow Robbie had managed to steal the watch by himself. He was the only person, other than herself, who had seen it on the train.

Spike mentioned that Robbie had been a magician. Was it possible that he had used some trick to take the watch out of her palm without her knowledge?

At the end of the day, she realized she'd been thinking over the pocket watch for too long. Whether Robbie had the watch or not, or if he'd stolen it or it was rightfully his—she'd focus on that tomorrow.

Right now, she had a whole evening to actually enjoy the celebration that Edwin had been an integral part of as mayor, and which had captivated her beloved hometown for the better part of a week.

It would be icing on the cake, though, if they could end the festival by returning Collin Malloy's watch to the citizens of Silver Peak.

Edwin and Sadie walked into the newly restored lobby of the opera house. It hummed with voices and anticipation as the crowd prepared for the movie showing in the auditorium.

Edwin leaned toward her. "Would you like some popcorn?"

Sadie smiled. "Popcorn sounds great."

Edwin went to join the line that was snaking its way across the lush, patterned carpet. The rich, buttery smell of fresh popcorn made her mouth water. She glanced around the lobby, which was a perfect replica of how it had looked in its heyday. In fact, it was difficult to believe, as with her excursion on the train, that she hadn't stepped back in time.

Was this how the lobby looked to Collin Malloy during his many concerts here? Things had probably become threadbare and worn in the 1930s, a far cry from its gaudy splendor at the end of the century, but since Malloy was born in one of the poorest neighborhoods in Denver, even the opera house at its most run-down might have seemed like a palace. Besides, it was the scene of his debut, his great triumph before taking on the bright lights of Hollywood. The opera house must have been a truly spectacular place in his mind.

Edwin approached, pulling her from her reverie. "Let's go grab our seats. I overheard at the concession stand that they're expecting a sold-out show."

The lights were dimmed for atmosphere but were still bright enough that she could easily follow the aisle toward the stage. They edged down one row of seats to the middle, but people were already starting to fill in the empty chairs around them.

Edwin set their popcorn on the floor and helped Sadie out of her coat. As he folded it over the seat, it gave a sharp crackle.

"What was that?" He sat beside her and scooped the refreshment tray off the floor.

"Oh! It's a letter." In all her concern over Theo, she'd forgotten the letter she'd tucked into her jacket pocket.

A steady stream of well-wishers stopped by Edwin's seat to say hello and to congratulate him on a lovely week of festivities. Sadie smiled and commented when appropriate, but it was obvious that Edwin was in his element as the town's mayor, chatting with the townspeople.

It would be all right if she sneaked a glance at that letter. She withdrew it from her jacket pocket and made her way to the powder room.

For once there was no line for the ladies' room, but even if there had been, a small dressing area offered a comfortable place to rest.

Sadie sank onto a velvet sofa and opened the yellowed envelope. It had been slit open at the top at some point in its existence. She withdrew the fragile letter and carefully unfurled the piece of paper.

It was written in a feminine hand, but the writing was so shaky and faded that it was difficult to read. She pulled the letter closer and squinted.

Dearest John,

You do not know me, and it breaks my heart that I do not know you. I have no right to write this letter, but they tell me I am dying, so this is my last chance.

I am your mother. I do not deserve the title, but it is still the truth. Your father, Collin, and I were deeply in love, but our lives were complicated and we could not be together in the way we wanted. He convinced me to give you up until we could sort out our lives, so the scandal would not ruin our careers. I always intended to come back for you, but then Collin died, and everything fell apart.

My excuses are not enough, I know. But I wanted, more than once, to reach out to you and let you know that I thought of you every day, and I hope that, despite my failings, you have had a good life so far.

I hope you can forgive me.

Your mother,
Elizabeth Schneider

Sadie gasped and sat for a moment, lost in thought, then snatched up the envelope. It was postmarked from Los Angeles, California, in 1972.

She stared at the name *Collin* in the middle of the letter. Could it be? If this letter were written to John Smith, Robert Smith's father, and John's father was named Collin…

Surely it must be Collin Malloy. It would explain so much—Robert's resemblance, why he had most likely taken the watch.

But who was Elizabeth Schneider? Sadie had not seen that name in her biography of Collin Malloy, nor in the list of starlets Collin had dated.

She pulled out her phone and typed "Elizabeth Schneider Collin Malloy" into Google's search bar. The search results were all pages dedicated to Malloy, which held no mention of Elizabeth Schneider.

Sadie turned back to the letter. Elizabeth and Collin had been worried the scandal would ruin their careers. *Both* of their careers. If the Collin in the letter was really Collin Malloy, then John Smith had to have been born in 1933 or earlier. Not many women had careers in the thirties. Had Elizabeth been an actress?

She typed "Elizabeth Schneider 1930s actress" into Google, and nearly fell off her chair.

The first result was the Wikipedia page for Betty Bright.

Sadie clicked it, and read in the first few lines that Betty Bright's real name was Elizabeth Schneider.

She remembered a few lines from the gossip column that Violet McKay had e-mailed her. Betty Bright had undergone surgery in 1933, but it was for an appendectomy. Had it been a ruse? Had she disappeared to have a baby, as women sometimes did in that era, and then given the child away?

And those lines from "The Mother Lode" column in the *Post-Gazette*. Collin Malloy had been seen in the company of a starlet who shone *brightly*. Of course!

Sadie felt a jolt of energy move through her. Here, at last, was the final piece of the puzzle. Or at least, nearly final.

She couldn't stay in the restroom much longer. The movie would be starting, and Edwin would wonder where she was. Sadie folded the letter up with shaking hands and left the restroom, carefully making her way down the aisle to her seat.

"Excuse me. Sorry. Excuse me," she whispered as she pushed past the other patrons to their seats in the middle of the row.

"Everything okay?" Edwin helped her into her seat and handed over a box of popcorn.

"Yes, fine." Her mind was buzzing.

The movie screen lit up with old newsreel footage, and the scratchy voice of the narrator detailed the victorious Hollywood career of Collin Malloy. Sadie leaned forward in her seat, all her senses focused on the details flashing past in black and white.

"Hollywood mourned the death of the great tenor Collin Malloy today, as he was laid to rest in Forest Lawn cemetery. Dignitaries from around the world sent their condolences."

The footage showed a funeral cortege winding its way through a cemetery, stopping at lovely small chapel.

"Here we see Hollywood's best and brightest come to say goodbye to their favorite opera and film star," the narrator intoned. A parade of Hollywood stars walked past the cameras on their way into the chapel—Clark Gable, Marie Dressler, Janet Gaynor, Robert Taylor...

Betty Bright, draped in a veil, clinging to a stout older woman for support. Her mother, perhaps?

The narrator said nothing in particular about any of the stars flashing by, and merely called off their names like the most famous roll call in the history of cinema. Then the film wound to a close, the camera closing in on a wreath laid across Malloy's coffin.

The screen dimmed, and a few seconds later the title card for *Merrily We Roll* flashed across it. The movie Collin Malloy and Betty Bright made together.

Sadie had never seen one of Betty Bright's movies before, but as she watched the energetic young blonde on screen, she felt tears prick at the back of her eyes. Betty was beautiful and charming, and her chemistry with Collin Malloy was electric. Watching them together, it was easy to see how an attachment could have developed.

And so much of both of them could be seen in Robert. Collin's eyes and smile, Betty's charm and grace. Watching them on screen together was almost more than she could bear.

She remembered the photo of Betty Bright hanging in the display in her shop, and a sudden certainty shot through her. Sadie stood.

"Sadie?" Edwin whispered. "What's wrong?"

She grabbed her coat. She had to get to the shop, because the final proof was waiting there, on display for the whole town to see.

"I've got to go." She apologized her way back down the row, with Edwin close on her heels.

"Sadie. Sadie!" His urgent whisper deepened into an exclamation as they reached the lobby. "What is it? Are you feeling all right?"

"I feel better than I have all week," she exclaimed. Her blood pounded in her ears, making her dizzy. "Come with me. We've got to go to the Antique Mine."

24

Sadie raced across the street to the Antique Mine, dodging the Dumpster and the barricades that Fleagle Construction had left in front of Spike's shop, her heart pounding with each step. She had to get the last piece of the puzzle to be sure of herself, to be certain that she was correct. Behind her, Edwin's footsteps thudded on the pavement. He said nothing but followed close on her heels.

At the front door of the Antique Mine, she fitted the key in the lock and opened the door. Then she flipped on the light and dashed inside.

"Sadie—" Edwin's voice sounded tired and carried a rare hint of exasperation. "Can't you tell me what's going on?"

"Here." Sadie pulled the picture of Betty Bright off the wall. "I needed to see this photo." She peered closely at Betty. "That's not a sock she's knitting. That's a baby's bootie."

Edwin drew close and looked over her shoulder. "Okay, so?"

"This clinches it!" Her heart leaped. "Robert Smith stole the pocket watch."

"I don't understand." Edwin pulled up a stool and sat down, withdrawing his handkerchief from his pocket. "How does this photograph tell you all that?"

"Because he's Collin Malloy's grandson." She flipped the frame over, removed the photo, and showed Edwin the caption on the back. "This picture was taken on the set of *Merrily We Roll*, the movie we were just watching. The one she starred in with Collin Malloy." This image—Betty knitting for the baby she would soon have—was a private moment, known only to a handful of people involved, but thanks to a nosy photographer, it had been captured and held for decades. "I think they became romantically involved, and Robert Smith is the son of the child from that relationship."

Edwin's blue eyes widened. "I'm still not seeing how all these pieces fit together."

Sadie laid the photograph and the frame on the counter and took the letter out of her purse. "I found this letter in a box of trash that Robert Smith left out behind Spike's shop."

Edwin's eyebrows raised. "You went through his trash?"

"I know, I know." She unfolded it and set it before Edwin. "Just read it."

Like her, Edwin had to squint to read Betty's shaky, feeble handwriting. "I still don't understand," he said after he finished. "How are you so sure that Robert Smith is related to Collin Malloy?"

"Because Betty Bright is just a stage name. Her real name was Elizabeth Schneider." She pointed at the letter. "This Elizabeth Schneider. While the gossip columns reported that Betty Bright had a ruptured appendix, she had really gone to the hospital to have her baby. Robert said his father, John, grew up in an orphanage. In this letter, you can see that Betty Bright put her son in an orphanage. She expected to adopt him back out, but then shortly after this Collin Malloy passed away."

She paused, struck by a thought. Why hadn't Betty Bright adopted her son anyway? Was it the stigma of being a single mother that worried her? Or had something happened to her? She hadn't mentioned her reasons in her letter, so perhaps they would never know.

"There are still some loose ends," she mused. "Like why Betty didn't adopt her son and how Robert knew to find the pocket watch on the train. The important thing, though, is that he did take the watch, possibly because he thinks it's rightfully his."

"And it might be," Edwin said, his cautious legal mind at work. "So what do we do now?"

Sadie reached out and squeezed his hand. "I think the most important thing right now is to talk to Robert Smith. What time is it? Is the movie over?"

Edwin glanced at his watch. "There's probably another half hour to go, and then the Skylarks will finish the evening with a short concert."

"Perfect. I hope Robert will be there." She squeezed Edwin's hand again. "Sorry I rushed out of the opera house like that. I just needed to see this picture of Betty once more, to prove to myself that I was right." She picked up the photo. "I'll bring this along. If Robert has no idea what his grandmother looked like, it's time they met."

Edwin led her out of the shop. She flipped off the lights and locked the front door, and they strolled together, arm in arm, back across the street to the opera house. The marquee lights sparkled dazzlingly against the inky night sky, and Sadie breathed in the crisp, cold air.

When they reentered the opera house, they decided just to lean up against the back wall. There was something a little magical about watching a movie this way. She could see the movie screen, the proscenium arch, and the entire audience illuminated by the flickering black-and-white darkness.

Merrily We Roll reached its romantic conclusion, with Collin Malloy sweeping Betty Bright dramatically into his arms, and the final title credit rolled.

As the house lights came up and the audience applauded, the Skylarks took the stage. They played a rousing rendition of "Home, Sweet Home," as the audience clapped along.

Edwin leaned over. "I'm supposed to go up and say a few words."

She squeezed his arm. "Knock 'em dead!"

Edwin strode up the aisle as the Skylarks played the closing bars of the song.

Robert Smith was there, standing beside Spike. He'd told the truth about intending to come back to Silver Peak after his interview in Denver, then. She'd be able to catch him after the performance and answer all her lingering questions.

George ushered Edwin up to the microphone. The audience's applause died down, but everyone remained in their seats. It was good to see that no one got up to leave. People in Silver Peak liked Edwin, and they respected him. Sadie's heart glowed with pride.

"Back in 1931," Edwin began, "Silver Peak faced its most daunting task—picking up the pieces as we descended into the Great Depression. Now, decades later, we celebrate and honor the achievements made during the depths of the greatest financial crisis our country has ever seen. We honor our town's victory over defeat. We cherish the relics of the past, and we give them new life in our time, because we know that our history has profound meaning and truth."

The audience burst into applause. Sadie smiled so widely her cheeks hurt.

"I want to thank our local community for supporting this weeklong celebration. I'd like to especially thank the Skylarks, whose music has provided a wonderful soundtrack to our festivities this week. Thank you, too, to the local merchants who have banded together to make this a special week. As in the past, Silver Peak pulled together in the present and the results have been marvelous. I am proud to call Silver Peak home and grateful to serve as your mayor. Thank you and good night."

The audience clapped once more, and Edwin descended from the stage and returned to Sadie's side at the back of the auditorium.

The Skylarks launched into song and played half a dozen vintage numbers before taking a bow. The evening was over.

People began leaving the theater, streaming up the aisle. On stage, the Skylarks were packing up their instruments.

It was time.

She and Edwin inched their way up the aisle against the flow of traffic, Edwin greeting people as they passed. As Sadie stepped onto the stage, the spotlight was shut off, as were the special stage lights. The house lights bathed the stage in much more natural tones, and the Skylarks, Edwin, and everyone scurrying around backstage lost their ethereal glow.

Sadie strode toward Robert Smith, who was putting his bass guitar back into its case. He looked up at her and smiled.

Sadie decided there was no point dancing around her question. She drew herself up as tall as possible and said, "Robbie, where's the diamond pocket watch?"

He turned ashen, all the blood draining from his face. He made a sudden movement as though he intended to flee, but Spike stepped up beside him, holding Robert steady by placing his hand on Robert's arm. Edwin moved to Robert's other side.

"Robbie, answer the question." Spike's voice was a hoarse rumble.

The other Skylarks were glancing their way, clearly interested in what was going on. Sadie hadn't meant this to be quite so dramatic. She motioned for the three men to follow her and walked backstage.

Robert trailed behind her, his arm still firmly clamped in Spike's grip. Edwin shadowed them both, making it impossible for Robert to turn around and run.

When they had gained the privacy of a quiet, darkened corner, Sadie took a deep breath and tried again. "Where's the watch?"

He looked from Spike to Edwin and back, then sagged. "How did you know it was me?"

"I thought at first that I had just dropped the watch," she admitted. "When the lights went out, I stumbled, and you helped me up. When the light came back on, the watch—and you—were both gone." She took a breath. "After that, it was a lot of little things. I found your fake glasses on the train. You were seen talking to Darcy Burke, who noticed you were wearing a wig. And you were so familiar to me. Even taking your resemblance to Collin Malloy into account. It had to be the mysterious man sitting next to me who took the watch, and that man had to be you."

Robert stared at the ground for a long moment, then cleared his voice. His lips trembled slightly as he began. "You're right, I stole it. You see, I was in a fix back in LA. I had gambled a lot and racked up some heavy losses. I was desperate for money. So I was ripping through my apartment, trying to find anything of value."

He closed his eyes and leaned his head back against the wall. "I had this box of old papers my father left me when he died. Research on his parents. His biological parents. He had this crazy idea he was the child of famous movie stars. No one ever believed him, but he had stacks and stacks of research on them. There was an old letter in there his mother wrote him just before she died, the only time he ever heard from her. She mentioned his father's name was Collin, so he'd decided that Collin was Collin Malloy. I mean, sure, we both looked a bit like him, but that doesn't mean anything. Anyway, one of the articles he had on this guy mentioned a diamond pocket watch that had gone missing in Silver Peak." He turned and gave Spike an apologetic look. "And I knew exactly where that was.

"My dad had made a bunch of notes all over the article, about some train engineer and gangsters. He thought maybe the watch was in the train somewhere, that the engineer had hidden it. Like I said, I thought my dad was crazy about all this stuff, but that idea stuck in my head.

"My theater tour ended last Friday in Denver, so I called Spike to see if I could come stay with him while I searched for a job, and he mentioned he was going on this fancy old-fashioned train ride. Well, how could I pass up that chance? What if the watch *was* on the train? So I conveniently forgot to turn in my costume from the play and drove up that night without telling anyone. I snuck onto the train, careful to avoid Spike the whole night, and found an empty seat."

Robert looked bleakly at Sadie. "And then you found that watch. I couldn't believe it. It was like it was meant to be. I used an old sleight-of-hand trick I learned as a magician to take it from you when you fell. I know I shouldn't have—but I owed a lot of people a lot of money."

"How did you disappear into the crowd?" Sadie asked. "Was that a magician's trick too?"

"No, just me moving fast. I grabbed the watch and slipped up the aisle. I knocked my glasses off in the process, but I couldn't stop to pick them up. When the lights came back on, I was several feet away already, and in the disorientation, I was able to squeeze past people and get off the train a second or two later."

"What did you do with the watch?" Edwin spoke for the first time since the end of his speech. His expression was impassive, his voice authoritatively judicial.

"I kept it. I couldn't bring myself to sell it, for some reason." Robert put his hand in his pocket and drew out the watch. Thousands of prisms danced off the brilliant surface, sending rainbows of color around the darkened backstage. "When I saw the inscription to Malloy from the people of Silver Peak, well, it got to my conscience." He laughed without mirth, then looked at Edwin. "You're the mayor. Since this watch belongs to Silver Peak, I should probably give it to you."

He held out the watch, and after a second of hesitating, Edwin accepted it. "Thank you." He closed his hand carefully around the priceless gold watch.

"What about all your gambling debts?" Sadie asked.

"Spike paid them." Robert shot a grateful glance at his friend. "He knew I was in a bad way, and he lent me the money to pay everyone off. He had just inherited some cash, and he offered to help me out. Now that I have a job waiting for me in Denver, I know I can pay him back. Well..." He looked down again. "Unless I'm going to jail."

Sadie looked at Edwin, pleading silently with him. He nodded.

"I don't think that will be necessary," he said. "You returned the watch, so no harm has been done."

Robert covered his face with one trembling hand, taking a moment to compose himself. He cleared his throat. "Thank you. I'm so sorry I took it."

They stood silently for a long moment, and then Sadie remembered the photo of Betty Bright in her hand. She held it out toward Robert. "Do you know this woman?"

"I think so. That's Betty Bright, right? She's the one my father thought was related to us."

"It is." Sadie gave him a warm smile. "And your father was right. She's your grandmother."

He looked sharply up at her. "Wait, so does that mean he was right about Collin Malloy too?"

"Yes. Betty Bright and Collin Malloy were romantically involved. Shortly after the film wrapped, the gossip columns announced that Betty had her appendix out and was spending a couple of months recovering, but really she had a baby. Collin convinced her to give the baby to an orphanage, but Betty hoped they'd marry and she'd be able to adopt her baby back. Unfortunately, Collin died, and Betty never claimed her son. Your father."

Her voice caught in her throat. Poor Betty. She shouldn't be judged too harshly for what she'd done. She must have felt so scared and alone when Collin died.

She pulled the letter from her pocket and handed it to him. "I'm sorry I read this," she said quietly, "but I needed to know more about you."

Robert snatched the letter from her hand. "I thought I'd lost it! Where did you find this?"

"In a box of trash behind Spike's apartment." She blushed and shot Spike an apologetic look. He shook his head dismissively, but his attention was focused on his friend.

He opened the letter and read it again. "Elizabeth Schneider—Betty Bright. Collin Malloy. I can't believe my father was right." Robert sighed.

Sadie bit her lip and gave Edwin a sideways glance. "Actually, you could argue that as Collin Malloy's grandson, the watch rightfully belongs to you..."

But Robert was already adamantly shaking his head. "No. It belongs to the town. I don't want it anymore." He lifted the letter and one side of his mouth crooked up. "Besides, I doubt this letter is enough proof for me to make that kind of claim."

"It's proof enough for me," Sadie said quietly.

Robert gave her his first real smile that night. "And for me."

25

Theo lounged on the couch, his stocking feet pointing toward the television. "I can't believe that after all that research, we never figured out where Collin Malloy's pocket watch was."

Sadie wandered into the living room from the kitchen and shared a smile with Edwin. Until he told her it was okay to tell others about the watch, she'd kept the matter between herself, Spike, and Edwin. "Well, at least we tried. And Sara won the essay contest! Free dinner at Sophia's! That should make us feel better."

"Yeah, but I am still disappointed about the watch." Theo sniffed the air appreciatively. "What are you making, Grandma? Smells good."

"I'm making roasted chicken and root veggies, plus mashed potatoes." Sadie smiled at her grandson. "Perfect for Sunday lunch and for injured ski heroes."

"Awesome." Theo turned his attention back to the television.

"Mom, how can I help?" Alice had been sitting with Edwin and Sara in the living room as Edwin kindled a fire in the hearth.

"Yeah, how can we help?" Sara asked.

Having her family all gathered at home after such a distressing weekend was the best thing Sadie could have hoped for. "Well, if you'd like to mash the potatoes, Alice, then Sara can set the table. We should be ready within half an hour."

"Did you hear that, Theo? Half an hour, and then the television goes off." Alice's voice held a warning note. "We'll eat in the dining room."

"Okay, Mom." Theo spoke distractedly, his attention obviously fixed on the television. Edwin sat back in the recliner and hoisted his feet up. Sadie chuckled and shook her head. She hoped the smell of food would be enough to pull them away from the game.

A knock sounded on the door, and Hank barked.

"I wonder who that could be." Sadie wiped her hands on her apron. "I invited Laura, but she knows better than to knock."

She opened the front door. Spike and Robert stood on the porch, their hands stuffed in their pockets. It was good to see them—she hadn't seen them at Campfire Chapel that morning and hadn't spoken to them since confronting Robert at the theater the night before.

"C'mon in!" she said, opening the door wide. "Are you boys here for Sunday lunch?"

Robert gave her a tentative smile. "I'm afraid not, Mrs. Speers. I was hoping to speak to you."

"Of course." Sadie motioned them in the door. "Excuse the crowd. I'm hosting lunch, as you can see." She led both men into the study, taking off her apron and draping it across the back of her chair. "Please, have a seat. How can I help you two?"

"Spike just drove me here," Robert said, shooting his friend a look of gratitude over his shoulder. "I wanted to ask you a question, but your store isn't open today."

Sadie's heart sank. "Have you changed your mind about the watch? Do you want it back?"

Robert's eyes widened. "No! Not at all. Ever since I took it from you that night, I knew I had no right to it. Knowing that Collin Malloy is my grandfather just strengthens my resolve. There's a reason the watch never made it to Hollywood and that it stayed here. There's a reason Collin Malloy never came back to claim it. When I read your granddaughter's essay in the *Sentinel*, I realized how much it meant to Silver Peak. It belongs here. It's a part of your town."

Sadie felt her throat tighten. "Thank you, Robbie. That means a lot. To all of us. Edwin's going to give the watch to the train station to be put on display so the whole town can enjoy the watch and what it means to our town."

"That sounds great." Robert pulled at his collar. "I have a favor to ask, though. I know this is a lot, because I've tried before and you said no."

Sadie drew her eyebrows together. What on earth was he talking about? "Go on."

"I tried to buy that photo of Betty Bright a few days ago, and you said it wasn't for sale." He looked at her, pleading with his best matinee idol expression. "You gave it to me last night to look at, but you didn't ask for it back. May I please purchase it?"

"I'm sorry, but no." Sadie laughed at his surprised expression. "You can't buy it, because I'm giving it to you. Betty was your grandmother. It's only fitting that she belongs to you. In fact, the sock she's knitting in that picture was actually a baby bootie for your father, so you see, in a way, it's a family photo."

"Really?" Robert's keen blue eyes filled with moisture. He blinked them rapidly. "Wow. I don't know what to say."

"Just say you'll buy her a decent frame, and that's enough for me."

"Thanks. I will. I promise I will." Robert turned to Spike. "I guess we should go. I need to leave in an hour or so anyway."

"Must you go? In a way, your roots are here." It was sad to bid him good-bye. He had been an enigma for so long, and now that she knew him for what he really was—a black sheep trying to make good—she wished he was staying in Silver Peak. "Besides, I'm making chicken and mashed potatoes, and there's more than enough for all of us."

"Thanks, but I'm due in Denver to start my new job tomorrow." He gave her his most charming smile. He really did look like his grandfather.

Both men rose, shuffling for the door.

"Oh, I want to give you one more thing," Sadie said as she stood. "You deserve to know your grandfather better." She walked over to her desk and grabbed the copy of Collin Malloy's biography, which she had placed haphazardly on a tottering stack of volumes. "I've been corresponding with Violet McKay, the author of this book, and I bet she'd like to know more about Collin's family. Take it. You can send her an e-mail and follow up. Maybe she can help you find out why Betty Bright was unable to adopt your father."

"I owe you so much." Robert accepted the book, running the palm of his hand over the cover. "In fact, I owe Silver Peak so much. When I came here, all I could think of was that I was in debt. I could only think of how to fix that, no matter what it took. This place and the people in it changed me."

"Oh, Robbie." From what Sadie could tell, this man had grown to middle age without knowing his true family, his true worth, or the depth of God's love. It was exhilarating to be standing here, watching him transform into the man he was meant to be. Sadie reached over and gave him a brief hug. Then, before Spike could protest, she hugged him too.

She ushered both men through the house, and they called out their good-byes. Sadie followed them both out onto the front porch.

"Come back and visit often," she told Robert. "If I come across any more Betty Bright or Collin Malloy memorabilia, I'll let you know."

Both men waved and headed toward Spike's beat-up old pickup truck. Sadie crossed her arms over her chest and watched until the truck faded into a tiny speck in the distance.

Then she went inside to enjoy Sunday lunch with the dearest people on earth, her heart full of thanksgiving.

"I can't believe this is the actual pocket watch that the people of Silver Peak gave Collin Malloy." Jack turned it carefully in his palm, his eyes wide. "Are you sure we can have it?"

"It belongs to the town," Edwin said. "It should become a part of the heritage of Silver Peak. As I said when I announced the treasure hunt, if the watch was found, it would go on display here in the station."

Sadie smiled at both men. Edwin had kindly let her accompany him to give the watch to Jack Fitzgerald.

"This is amazing," Jack said. "We'll make sure we show it off as much as it deserves, make the whole town proud, though I'm afraid we'll need to augment our security system now." He smiled. "By the way, who found it?"

Edwin shook his head. "They asked to remain anonymous."

Jack gave him a shrewd look, then switched his gaze to Sadie. "Uh-huh."

She raised her hands in a gesture of innocence and laughed.

"Don't give me that, Sadie. You were involved in this somehow. I can tell." Jack grinned at her.

Sadie laughed. "Well, I might have helped a little."

Jack laughed with her, but then his face fell. "I'm sorry again that we still haven't found the rest of your mugs and that coffee service," Jack replied. Embarrassment was plainly written across his face. "Please let us repay you."

"Oh, don't worry about that. I got those back," she replied briskly. "I think you must have miscounted. Once I got that one box back, everything was there."

She said a silent prayer asking forgiveness for the fib. There was no need for Darcy to be branded as a thief, especially to her uncle.

"Oh. Well, great." Jack's eyebrows knit together as though he was puzzled.

"No problem. That kind of thing happens at events all the time."

Edwin and Sadie watched as Jack tucked the pocket watch into the safe in his office, then bade him good-bye with one last promise to be in touch.

As she swung her Tahoe out of the parking lot and headed toward Arbuckle's, Hank Williams's "Hey, Good Lookin'" came on the radio. She turned it up loud and sang along boisterously, making Edwin laugh and join in.

Life was good. Edwin was wonderful. Silver Peak, with a little help from Sadie, had just regained an invaluable piece of its history and heritage. And a drifting young man had found his roots.

As the song wound to a close, she said a quick prayer of thanks. God was good, indeed.

About the Author

CAROLE JEFFERSON IS THE PEN NAME FOR A TEAM OF WRITERS who have come together to create the series Mysteries of Silver Peak. *Time Will Tell* was written by Lily George. Lily grew up devouring the books in her mother's bookstore and wrote for three hours each night after her family went to sleep. But she never dreamed that anyone would actually want to read her writing until she came up with the plot for *Captain of Her Heart*, her first inspirational Regency romance, which was published in 2012. It was followed by *The Temporary Betrothal* in 2012, *Healing the Soldier's Heart* in 2013, and *A Rumored Engagement* in 2014. This is her first book for Guideposts.

Read on for a sneak peek of another exciting book in Mysteries of Silver Peak!

A Code of Honor

SADIE SPEERS LEANED CLOSER TO THE FOURTEEN-YEAR-OLD GIRL and peered into her hazel eyes. "Want to borrow my garden trowel?"

Sara tilted her head, and her strawberry blonde hair fell over one shoulder. "What for, Grandma? We're going to church. Besides, it's December. Way too cold for gardening."

Sadie grinned. "Because that's the only way you can cake the eye shadow on any thicker than you already have."

Her granddaughter rolled her eyes and sighed, a gesture and sound reminiscent of her mother—Sadie's daughter—at that pubescent age. "It's called smoky eye, Grandma. People in the theater always wear dramatic makeup."

Amused, Sadie got up from her chair at the kitchen table and retrieved a small jar of coconut oil from the pantry. "What, and make us miss out on the opportunity to see your natural beauty?" She handed her the jar. "Here, this should take it off and let your true gorgeousness shine."

"Braces aren't natural or beautiful," the girl said with a metallic pout that seemed to emphasize her point, "which is why I was trying to take attention away from them and direct it to my eyes. Sleeping over at your house was fun until this morning."

Despite the protestations, Sara took the jar of coconut oil and went down the hall to the bathroom to remove the makeup.

Hank, Sadie's golden retriever, stood at the entrance to the hall for a moment, as if trying to decide whether to follow. After a brief hesitation, he settled himself under the breakfast table, perhaps in hopes of snagging a treat from Sadie's plate.

She checked her watch. There was still plenty of time before church. While she waited for Sara, she could finish her coffee and check her favorite Internet blogs on her laptop computer. First up was the *Chatterbox*, Silver Peak's news-slash-gossip column, whose anonymous author dispensed information about births, deaths, and local events. Whoever it was that wrote the blog seemed to have access to all the latest news—and sometimes bits of gossip that turned out to be nothing more than friction starters—but so far no one had been able to figure out whom he or she might be. One of these days, Sadie might set her sights on unmasking the person who scoured the community for reportable tidbits.

Done with that for now, she plucked a tiny piece of leftover bacon from her plate and passed it to Hank under the table, where his tail *whack-whack-whacked* against a chair leg. When no more was forthcoming, he went down the hall in search of Sara, perhaps to beg a taste of coconut oil.

Sadie switched to the other blog she'd been reading regularly for the past several years. The Domestic Miss was written by Donelle Enzer, a community servant in southwestern Virginia.

A Code of Honor

The banner over the blog came from Matthew 25:40: "...*whatever you did for one of the least of these brothers and sisters of mine, you did for me.*" Donelle took that sentiment to heart, helping people at Heritage Road Church and in her small Appalachian town. In addition, she made her living in a way that was similar to Sadie's antique restoration and dealing. Donelle found salvageable items, whether antique or not, fixed them up, and sold them to locals and tourists.

It was while searching for a quick and easy method to remove finish from chair rungs that Sadie had stumbled upon the Web site seven years ago and discovered that Donelle and she shared many interests and similarities. They both lived in the mountains, loved the outdoors, and were involved in their communities.

They had connected after Sadie began replying regularly in the comments section beneath the blogs, and the friendship grew from there. Before long, they were e-mailing privately, sometimes asking advice of each other on restoring an artifact and other times just to offer an encouraging word.

So it was a given that when Sadie went east a couple of years ago to hike a portion of the Appalachian Trail, her friend invited her to church and served her lunch afterward. Though seeing each other for the first time, it had seemed as though they'd already met like this a thousand times before.

That was when Sadie saw for herself the poor living conditions of many people in the poverty-stricken community and how much they relied on the help of Heritage Road Church.

Sadie adjusted the screen and dug in, almost certain of coming away with a feel-good blog message and a smile. Unfortunately, the first sentence nixed that possibility.

Please pray for our church and especially for the people who were hurt when the roof collapsed yesterday.

Sadie's hand went to her throat as if to catch the gasp the words elicited. Donelle and her fellow church members had been feeding the poor and homeless when the weight of melting snow had collapsed the ancient roof. Donelle's husband had been among the injured, but the Domestic Miss was equally concerned about the underprivileged people of the community who'd had the misfortune to be standing under the falling timber and plaster and who would be affected by the church's inability to serve them until the damage was repaired.

"...If it's repaired," Donelle had written, underscoring the word *if*. The church, which Sadie knew struggled to make do on its limited resources, might have to close its doors after this devastating event.

Sadie calculated the time. It would be two hours later in Virginia, but Donelle was not likely to be going to church today. She picked up the phone to call her friend and get the rest of the details.

"Thanks so much for calling, Sadie. I can't tell you how much that means to me." Donelle went on to tell Sadie about what had happened to the church and those who had been injured. After hearing of the losses, both tangible and physical, Sadie wanted to help, but the damage was much bigger than her wallet.

"Let me think on this," she told her friend. "There must be something we can do. In the meantime, I'll add you and your community to our church's prayer list." They said their good-byes and ended the call.

Sara returned, Hank on her heels, after Sadie hung up the phone. In Sadie's opinion, the improvement was enormous, but Sara's mouth tugged downward.

"There," she said, sounding bored. "My eyes have no drama now. They're boring…just like the rest of my life."

In general, Sadie made it a practice not to lecture her grandchildren, preferring a more lighthearted approach. But today the irony of Sara's words struck at her heart.

"Be grateful," she said softly. "There are some people who wish they didn't have so much drama in their lives."

A scuttling noise skittered overhead. All around Sadie and her family, faces tipped upward, but this time it wasn't in prayer or worship. Children giggled. Adults frowned. Even Pastor Don Sweeting paused in his Sunday-morning message to joke that it sounded as though some creature in the attic was trying to get closer to hear God's word this morning.

Sadie reached over and grasped Sara's arm to remind her to stay focused on the preaching. Sara's mother Alice and older brother Theo were just as distracted, but Sadie wasn't about to reach across her granddaughter to nudge them.

Besides, Sadie herself was having a hard time staying focused, though not because of the presence of a hyperactive critter in the attic. Her thoughts kept returning to Donelle, her husband's back injury, and the plight of the Appalachian people who needed their church's assistance.

The scratching sounds quieted, then continued again, but louder. Sadie glanced over at Edwin who gave her a look that seemed to say, "I'll check it out."

After closing prayer, she followed Edwin out of the sanctuary to the attic door and waited at the bottom while he maneuvered up the narrow stairs to investigate. Along with her, Alice, Theo, and Sara, a handful of other church members gathered around to satisfy their curiosity. Even Teddy Wellington, a corporate CEO who dressed the part with expensive suits and handmade cuff links, lingered to see what had been causing the ruckus.

Sara, the animal lover and future veterinarian, wanted to go up with Edwin, but Theo stopped her with a reminder that too many people would only frighten the creature into hiding. Alice grasped her daughter's hand in an effort to calm her fears for the animal.

"Don't hurt it!" the teen called up to Edwin, and he quickly assured her that he had no desire to harm one of God's creatures.

After a short delay, Pastor Don joined them and a few other curious people who had gathered to learn the source of the noise. At 6'2" the former rodeo star and retired police captain could appear intimidating to those who didn't know him, but his heart was pure gold. About four years younger than Sadie's own sixty-two years, he had the wisdom of someone much older. His wife Jeanne often claimed he was as sweet as his chocolate skin.

"Any luck?" Don asked.

"No, I can't find it," Edwin called from upstairs.

Sara paced the floor beside the watchers below. "What if the little guy is sick or hurt? We need to find him."

"Whatever it is," Sadie told her granddaughter to ease her worry, "it's just hiding from Edwin's big feet."

Edwin appeared at the entrance. "I heard that." He motioned to Sadie. "You've got to see this. Don, you too."

The pastor stepped away. "I'm afraid I have somewhere to go in a few minutes." He motioned to Sadie. "But you're more than welcome to go up."

Edwin held out his hand to assist her as she reached the top of the stairs. Behind him were two piles, one consisting of old cupboards, a couple of rough-but-salvageable doors, and even an old kitchen sink, apparently all stored up here after the church had been renovated. However, it was the other pile farther back in the attic that captured their attention. Clothes, furniture, hand tools, appliances, dishes, toys, and even a horse bridle.

"Where did all of this come from?"

"Your guess is as good as mine."

The antiques hunter in her came alive, and it was all she could do to keep from digging in and sorting through it right away. None of it appeared to be from this millennium.

Don called to them, and she walked over to the doorway to tell him and the others about their find.

"You won't believe all the great stuff up here," Sadie said. "It's an antiquer's dream. We should bring it down and go through it."

The pastor rubbed a hand over his close-cropped black hair. "Now's not a good time. There's a committee meeting this afternoon. Let's wait until we have the time and room—not to mention a plan—to sort it and decide what to do with it."

He was right, but Sadie hated to abandon the find without poking through at least one of the boxes. The varied collection of items had her wondering if perhaps these were the remnants of an abandoned yard sale. She opened a cardboard box filled with books and thumbed through the dusty titles.

Christy, by Catherine Marshall. A James Bond novel. Oddly enough, a copy of *One Flew Over the Cuckoo's Nest*, which she assumed had been mindlessly tossed in with the others. And an assortment of Bible study guides. But the real prize lay wedged between a copy of *To Kill a Mockingbird* and a packet of salvation tracts: a leather-bound Bible complete with embossed cover and gold-edged pages.

Sadie gently caressed the worn binding and imagined how it might look when restored to its full beauty. Carefully, so as not to crease the pages, she opened to the color-printed illustrations and admired the detailed artwork and crisp colors that had not faded over the years. The old-fashioned typeface and quaint pictures reminded her of her own grandmother's Bible of many years ago, and a sweet reminiscence settled over her like a breeze through the curtains while napping on a warm summer day.

The book had held up well in the widely varying temperatures and humidities of the church's attic, though Colorado's dry climate probably had helped preserve it. Naturally, her next thoughts turned to the best way to remove a couple of dark spots from the—

Edwin laid a hand on her shoulder. "Easy there, Sadie. You're going to leave drool marks on that nice Bible."

As quickly as she had lost herself in the book's beautiful craftsmanship, she snapped out of her glaze-eyed stare. If it had been anyone else to catch her going off to la-la land, she might have been embarrassed. But Edwin, the high school sweetheart she'd recently been reunited with after so many years apart, understood her passion for all items that were rich with history.

Sara's voice drifted up to them. "I got a trap from the toolshed behind the church."

Reluctantly, Sadie drew her thoughts back to the present. Until this moment, she'd forgotten about the animal that had prompted Edwin up here in the first place. "Well, come on up," she said. "Just watch out for nails and rough boards."

Her granddaughter carefully placed the humane trap in a corner where she thought the animal might feel comfortable taking the peanut-buttered-bread bait from the church's pantry. "I'll check again in a little while, and if it works we can release him into the woods where he belongs."

Proud of her granddaughter's big heart, Sadie gave her a warm hug. "Good plan."

Still clutching the box of books, they went back to the main floor where she and Edwin—Sadie more so than Edwin—excitedly told the group of onlookers what they'd found. Rather than risk unintended damage from curious fingers, she elected not to open the box to display its contents.

Elderly Harry Polmiller leaned in to hear what she was saying. "That sounds like what we collected for missions back when this church was called Montcrest Memorial. Lanford was there. He probably remembers it too."

In his early nineties, Harry was the oldest member of Campfire Church and certainly a longtime member of the community.

"Why didn't it ever ship out?" Sadie had to assume that, since the box was still here and not in the hands of needy people. And if anyone knew anything about the contents of the attic, Harry would. "We collected all that stuff to send to a needy village in Africa, but some of the members raised a squabble over whether it was better to help people so far away or let charity begin at home."

He paused to search his memory for more details about their attic find. While she waited for him to finish, the thought crossed her mind that, unfortunately, no one had benefited from this collection.

He shook his head sadly. "Eventually, disagreements between factions in the church brought it all to a standstill," he continued, "and it was decided that shipping all that heavy stuff overseas would be too expensive, anyway. So it was packed away and forgotten. Until now. Gosh, that must have been... 1970? Something like that."

Sadie wracked her brain, trying to piece together the history of the church building and how those items had come to exist all these years later. "Wait a minute. This building was slated for demolition about ten years ago. That's when Campfire Chapel acquired it and began renovations."

Harry Polmiller nodded in confirmation.

She remembered the lengths to which the members went to return the white clapboard building to its former glory. Even the bell in the steeple had its own crew of workers polishing the brass to a high gleam.

"Before that," she added, "it sat vacant for a long time, right? What about before then?"

Don and the others, clearly captivated, turned to the elderly gentleman to await the remainder of his recollections about the church's history.

A Code of Honor

Harry cleared his throat, obviously enjoying the attention. "Well, I can only tell you as far back as I know, being a member of Montcrest since I was born. The church had its ups and downs in membership, but when people started moving to Silver Peak in the nineties, we got more members than the church could hold. So they built a new church building down toward the valley and were so busy building and growing there that they didn't have time to do anything with this one."

Sara was among those listening raptly. "But why did you leave the church you were with for so long?"

As soon as she said it, Sadie cringed a little. Even Theo, who could be clueless sometimes, gave her a nudge. Sometimes politics and factions caused churches to splinter, and if that was the case for Harry, she didn't want him to feel put on the spot. "I'm sure Mr. Polmiller—"

"It was getting harder for me to navigate the drive to the new Montcrest," Harry said, providing an answer that eased her concerns. "So when Campfire Chapel reopened the doors, it felt like I was coming home."

"And we're very glad to have you here," Don said and clapped Harry on the back. "Thank you for sharing that with us."

With the noon meal calling, the group started to say their good-byes, and Alice asked if she'd be joining the family for lunch, but Sadie couldn't let everyone leave just yet. Especially Don. Not until she addressed the plight of her blogger friend's church in southwestern Virginia.

"Before you go, I need to get your okay on something," she said, blurting the idea that had hit her only a second ago.

~ 239 ~

"There's a friend of mine in Virginia whose church and community are in serious trouble."

Don nodded. "The ones you asked us to pray for during church?"

"Yes. Since the things in the attic were originally intended for missions anyway, what if we donated the usable items to Heritage Road Church? Anything that's too large to ship can be sold and the money donated." The more she thought about it, the better she liked the idea. "The same could go for any antiques and valuables. What do you think?"

Don nodded, and the others quickly agreed that it would be better to give the items to people who could use them than let them continue to sit in the attic, gathering dust. "Sounds good," he said, sealing the arrangement.

"Great!" Edwin said. "You can start by fixing up the Bible in that box. It should bring a pretty penny."

That was precisely what she had in mind. Her hands nearly itched to get started returning the book to its former luster. Considering how taken she was with it, she might even buy it for herself to admire whenever she pleased.

She quickly rounded up a few volunteers to help with sorting and cleaning. Unfortunately, the soonest they could use the fellowship hall was Sunday afternoon, two weeks from now. She tried to tamp down her impatience by reminding herself that the Appalachian church would need the money in a couple of weeks just as much as it needed help now. She couldn't wait to tell Donelle about her plan.

Read about the real-life inspiration behind Mysteries of Silver Peak by Jon Woodhams, Guideposts Books editor.

Discovering Silver Peak

I WALKED TO THE WINDOW OF MY NEW OFFICE AND PEERED DOWN at the yellow cabs and pedestrians twelve floors below. I could hear the horns honking, even this far up. I pinched myself, not quite believing I was working in Manhattan. My first day as a fiction editor for Guideposts Books. I'd been a book editor for years, but this was something new for me, creating a dynamic fiction series, pulling characters and plots from my imagination. Now that I needed to actually come up with an idea, the doubts crept in. Could I really do this job? Not just edit a book but create a whole fictional world? I said a quick prayer—a prayer for inspiration.

Many of Guideposts' fiction series have featured charming seaside towns and protagonists who use both their faith and their wits. I'd just come to New York from landlocked Colorado. Maybe a western location would resonate with our readers.

I picked up a magnet I'd stuck on my office bookshelf. It read *Leadville, Colorado: The Two-Mile-High City*. One of the first places I'd visited when I moved to Colorado Springs. One June day a friend and I decided to drive to Leadville, the highest incorporated city in the United States. My little car wheezed and gasped as it carried us from Colorado Springs's six thousand-foot elevation to Leadville's thin-aired 10,430 feet, passing herds of grazing buffalo and the silver mines that had fueled the area's boomtown days.

It was sunny but quite cool despite the time of year. We wheezed a bit ourselves as we walked the streets gunfighters like Doc Holliday had once trod. The views were beautiful and Leadville's rustic charms were irresistible. The brick buildings had been constructed at the height of the town's silver boom in the late 1800s, and even in varying states of disrepair, they still reflected the rich Victorian architecture of the era.

An old hardware store had been turned into an antiques mall and beautiful galleries had art depicting the rough-and-tumble days of the Old West. We passed the office of the *Herald Democrat*, Leadville's newspaper, published since the 1880s. Restaurants looked as if they might once have served hardscrabble miners.

Then we came to the Tabor Opera House. We poked our heads in. There was the sound of hammering. Workers called to one another across the old auditorium. A gray-haired woman with glasses welcomed us and offered to give us a tour.

We climbed up to the lighting catwalks. We stood on the stage where turn-of-the-century luminaries such as Houdini, John Philip Sousa and Sarah Bernhardt had performed. After giving a lecture there in 1882, the English wit Oscar Wilde visited a nearby saloon, "where I saw the only rational method of art criticism," he wrote. "Over the piano was printed a notice—'Please do not shoot the pianist. He is doing his best.'" We were breathless from the exertion at the high elevation, but our hostess was unfazed. She, almost single-handedly, it seemed, was spearheading the restoration of the historic structure.

At the end of the tour we thanked her and joked about how hard it had been to keep up with her.

She laughed. "I'm in my eighties, you know," she said. I was stunned. She looked much younger and had the energy of someone half her age. "I don't know how much longer I'll be able to keep working to fix up this old place, but I will as long as I can, and then I hope my daughter will take over...." She left it there.

Now, years later, as I remembered her passion for the place, I thought, *She could be the main character in the fiction series.* Not exactly her, but someone with her indomitable spirit, and the setting would be an old Western town with a colorful history. Thus was born Sadie Speers, the heroine of our new series *Mysteries of Silver Peak*. Instead of restoring an old opera house, Sadie runs an antique shop, but she's just as knowledgeable about her town as my tour guide was. She's the person everyone turns to with questions about its history and mysteries.

As the first *Silver Peak* book rolled off the presses I wondered, *Who was that woman we spoke to? Whatever happened to her?* I searched online. Lo and behold, front and center on the Tabor Opera House Facebook page was a photograph of our tour guide, Evelyn Livingston Furman.

There was also an obituary from the *Herald Democrat*. Mrs. Furman had died in February 2011, two months short of her ninety-eighth birthday. She was widely credited with saving the opera house. Not only had she overseen its restoration but she was the one who, in 1954, purchased the building to prevent it from being torn down. Today it's run by her daughter and son-in-law, just as she'd hoped.

Sadie Speers—like her real-life inspiration—is a woman with a passion for her town and its history. She puts that love to good use in each and every volume of this exciting series. I hope you'll find the books, and Sadie, as memorable and inspiring as Evelyn Furman was to me.

A Note from the Editors

We hope you enjoy Mysteries of Silver Peak, created by the Books and Inspirational Media Division of Guideposts, a nonprofit organization that touches millions of lives every day through products and services that inspire, encourage, help you grow in your faith, and celebrate God's love in every aspect of your daily life.

Thank you for making a difference with your purchase of this book, which helps fund our many outreach programs to military personnel, prisons, hospitals, nursing homes, and educational institutions. To learn more, visit GuidepostsFoundation.org.

We also maintain many useful and uplifting online resources. Visit Guideposts.org to read true stories of hope and inspiration, access OurPrayer network, sign up for free newsletters, download free e-books, join our Facebook community, and follow our stimulating blogs.

To learn about other Guideposts publications, including the best-selling devotional *Daily Guideposts*, go to ShopGuideposts.org, call (800) 932-2145, or write to Guideposts, PO Box 5815, Harlan, Iowa 51593.

SIGN UP FOR THE

Guideposts Fiction e-Newsletter

and stay up-to-date on the Guideposts fiction you love!

You'll get sneak peeks of new releases, hear from authors of your favorite books, receive special offers just for you …

AND IT'S FREE!

Just go to **Guideposts.org/newsletters** *today to sign up.*